Quickbooks

Step Guide to Financial Reporting for Small Business Owners

(Effortlessly Navigate and Optimize Quickbooks Online for Small Business Owners)

Gerald Delaney

Published By **Bengion Cosalas**

Gerald Delaney

All Rights Reserved

Quickbooks: Step Guide to Financial Reporting for Small Business Owners (Effortlessly Navigate and Optimize Quickbooks Online for Small Business Owners)

ISBN   978-1-7779502-2-4

No part of this guidebook shall be reproduced in any form without permission in writing from the publisher except in the case of brief quotations embodied in critical articles or reviews.

Legal & Disclaimer

The information contained in this book is not designed to replace or take the place of any form of medicine or professional medical advice. The information in this book has been provided for educational & entertainment purposes only.

The information contained in this book has been compiled from sources deemed reliable, and it is accurate to the best of the Author's knowledge; however, the Author cannot guarantee its accuracy and validity and cannot be held liable for any errors or omissions. Changes are periodically made to this book. You must consult your doctor or get professional medical advice before using any of the suggested remedies, techniques, or information in this book.

Upon using the information contained in this book, you agree to hold harmless the Author from and against any damages, costs, and expenses, including any legal fees potentially resulting from the application of any of the information provided by this guide. This disclaimer applies to any damages or injury caused by the use and application, whether directly or indirectly, of any advice or information presented, whether for breach of contract, tort, negligence, personal injury, criminal intent, or under any other cause of action.

You agree to accept all risks of using the information presented inside this book. You need to consult a professional medical practitioner in order to ensure you are both able and healthy enough to participate in this program.

Table Of Contents

Chapter 1: Editing Transactions

Edit an Invoice

Select the suitable bill from the listing of transactions, and then hit the "E" key to regulate it. By doing this, you may be able to edit the invoice's consumer data, services or products records, and other records in the Edit Invoice window.

Edit a Bill

Select the bill from the list of transactions and hit the "E" key to modify it. By doing so, the Edit Bill window will seem, allowing you to edit the bill's provider information, services or products information, and one-of-a-kind specifics.

Edit an Expense

To edit a charge, select the charge from the list of transactions and press the "E" key. This will open the Edit Expense window, wherein you could make changes to the account records, payee data, and one-of-a-kind info for the charge.

Edit a Check

Select the test from the listing of transactions, and then hit the "E" key to regulate it. By doing this, you may be able to edit the check's payee, amount, and one-of-a-kind details within the Edit Check window.

Edit a Sales Receipt

To edit a earnings receipt, select the income receipt from the list of transactions and press the "E" key. This will open the Edit Sales Receipt window, wherein you could make adjustments to the purchaser facts, products or services facts, and awesome records for the income receipt.

Edit a Purchase Order

To edit a buy order, pick out the purchase order from the list of transactions and press the "E" key. By doing so, the Edit Purchase Order field will appear, allowing you to edit the vendor facts, products or services facts, and one in every of a kind purchase order specifics.

Edit an Estimate

Select the estimate from the listing of transactions and hit the "E" key to regulate the estimate. By doing this, you may be able to edit the estimate's customer statistics, products or services records, and distinct specifics inside the Edit Estimate box.

Edit a Credit Memo

Editing a credit score score memo is as easy as deciding on it from the listing of transactions and urgent the "E" key. By doing this, you will be capable of edit the credit rating memo's client facts, products or services facts, and different specifics in the Edit Credit Memo container.

Edit a Refund Receipt

To edit a refund receipt, pick out the refund receipt from the list of transactions and press the "E" key. This will open the Edit Refund Receipt window, in which you can make adjustments to the consumer information, services or products records, and distinct information for the refund receipt.

Edit a Journal Entry

To edit a journal access, pick the mag get admission to from the listing of transactions and press the "E" key. This will open the Edit Journal Entry window, in which you could make modifications to the account records, debit and credit score rating quantities, and different records for the journal access.

Deleting Transactions

1.   Delete an Invoice: To delete an bill, choose the invoice from the listing of transactions and press the "D" key.

2.   Delete a Bill: To delete a bill, pick out out the invoice from the listing of transactions and press the "D" key.

3.   Delete an Expense: To delete an fee, choose out the price from the listing of transactions and press the "D" key.

four.   Delete a Check: To delete a test, pick out the take a look at from the listing of transactions and press the "D" key.

5.   Delete a Sales Receipt: To delete a income receipt, select the income receipt from the listing of transactions and press the "D" key.

6.   Delete a Purchase Order: To delete a buy order, pick the acquisition order from the listing of transactions and press the "D" key.

7.   Delete an Estimate: To delete an estimate, choose the estimate from the list of transactions and press the "D" key.

eight. Delete a Credit Memo: To delete a credit score memo, select out the credit score rating memo from the listing of transactions and press the "D" key.

9.   Delete a Refund Receipt: To delete a repayment receipt, pick out the refund receipt from the listing of transactions and press the "D" key.

10.   Delete a Journal Entry: To delete a mag get right of entry to, pick out out the mag get right of access to from the list of transactions and press the "D" key.

Saving Transactions

1.   Save a New Transaction: To hold a ultra-modern transaction, which includes an invoice or an expense, press the "Ctrl+S" keys to your keyboard. This will right now shop the transaction and upload it in your books.

2.   Save an Edited Transaction: To hold modifications made to an gift transaction, together with an edited bill or fee, press the "Ctrl+S" keys in your keyboard. This will keep the modifications and replace the transaction in your books.

three. Save a Transaction and Create Another: To keep a transaction and without delay create every other one, press the "Ctrl+Alt+S" keys for your keyboard. This will save the modern-day-day transaction and open a contemporary transaction shape if you want to fill out.

four. Save and Close a Transaction: To maintain a transaction and near the form, press the "Ctrl+Alt+C" keys on your keyboard. This will keep the transaction and near the form, taking you returned to the transaction list.

5.   Save and New: To save a transaction and right now create a ultra-modern one of the same type, press the "Ctrl+Alt+N" keys on your keyboard. This will maintain the modern transaction and open a new transaction form of the identical kind.

6.   Save and Next: To hold a transaction and pass to the next transaction in the listing, press the "Ctrl+Alt+Down Arrow" keys in your keyboard. This will keep the contemporary transaction and waft you to the following transaction in the listing.

7. Save and Previous: To keep a transaction and circulate to the previous transaction inside the list, press the "Ctrl+Alt+Up Arrow" keys for your keyboard. This will keep the cutting-edge transaction and flow into you to the preceding transaction within the listing.

eight. Save and Duplicate: To maintain a transaction and create a reproduction of it, press the "Ctrl+Alt+D" keys to your keyboard. This will shop the modern-day transaction and create a modern-day transaction form with all of the equal statistics as the genuine transaction.

9. Save and Print: To maintain a transaction and right away print it, press the "Ctrl+P" keys to your keyboard. This will maintain the transaction and open the print conversation field, allowing you to print the transaction proper now.

10. Save and Email: To preserve a transaction and right away electronic mail it to a consumer or provider, press the "Ctrl+E"

keys to your keyboard. This will store the transaction and open the e-mail form, allowing you to supply the transaction to the recipient.

Copying and Pasting Transactions

1.   Copy a Transaction: To duplicate a transaction, which include an bill or an value, pick out the transaction and press "Ctrl+C" to your keyboard. This will replica the transaction in your clipboard.

2.   Paste a Transaction: To paste a copied transaction, navigate to the preferred area, which incorporates the consumer's web web web page or the transaction list, and press "Ctrl+V" to your keyboard. This will paste the copied transaction and create a brand new transaction shape with all the same statistics as the particular transaction.

three. Paste a Transaction as a New Transaction: To paste a copied transaction as a trendy transaction, press "Ctrl+Alt+V" to your keyboard. This will paste the copied transaction as a new transaction, and you may edit any statistics that need to be modified.

four.   Paste a Transaction as a Bill: To paste a copied transaction as a bill, press "Ctrl+Shift+V" to your keyboard. This will paste the copied transaction as a cutting-edge day bill and let you edit any facts that want to be modified.

five.   Paste a Transaction as a Sales Receipt: To paste a copied transaction as a income receipt, press "Ctrl+Alt+Shift+V" on your keyboard. This will paste the copied transaction as a cutting-edge day earnings receipt and let you edit any info that want to be modified.

Navigation Shortcuts

Navigating Between Windows

1.   Switch to the Previous Window: To transfer to the preceding window, press "Ctrl+Tab" to your keyboard. This will take you to the closing window you had open.

2.   Switch to the Next Window: To transfer to the subsequent window, press "Ctrl+Shift+Tab" for your keyboard. This will take you to the subsequent window within the order they were opened.

3.   Open a New Window: To open a modern-day window, press "Ctrl+N" on your keyboard. This will open a present day-day browser tab or window, relying in your browser settings.

4.   Close the Current Window: To near the modern-day window, press "Ctrl+W" to your keyboard. This will near the modern tab or window.

5.   Maximize the Current Window: To maximize the current window, press "F11" on your keyboard. This will make the QuickBooks Online window entire-screen.

6.   Minimize the Current Window: To lessen the cutting-edge window, press "Windows key+Down Arrow" for your

keyboard. This will decrease the QuickBooks Online window to the taskbar.

7.   Restore the Current Window: To repair the present day window, press "Windows key+Up Arrow" for your keyboard. This will restore the QuickBooks Online window to its preceding duration.

Navigating Within a Window

1.   Move to the Next Field: To circulate to the following problem in a form, press the "Tab" key in your keyboard. This will flow your cursor to the following problem.

2.   Move to the Previous Field: To circulate to the preceding place in a form, press "Shift+Tab" for your keyboard. This will drift your cursor to the previous location.

Chapter 2: Jumping To Specific Fields

1.   Jump to the First Field in a Form: To leap to the primary area in a form, press "Ctrl+Alt+Shift+1" to your keyboard. This will bypass your cursor to the number one vicinity in the shape.

2.   Jump to the Second Field in a Form: To leap to the second area in a form, press "Ctrl+Alt+Shift+2" for your keyboard. This will move your cursor to the second one area within the form.

three. Jump to the Third Field in a Form: To jump to the 1/three subject in a shape, press "Ctrl+Alt+Shift+three" for your keyboard. This will circulate your cursor to the zero.33 situation within the shape.

four.   Jump to the Last Field in a Form: To jump to the final subject in a shape, press "Ctrl+Alt+Shift+L" to your keyboard. This will drift your cursor to the remaining subject inside the shape.

5.   Jump to the Memo Field: To bounce to the memo subject in a form, press "Ctrl+Alt+M" for your keyboard. This will flow into your cursor to the memo region inside the form.

6.   Jump to the Customer Field: To jump to the purchaser subject in a form, press "Ctrl+Alt+C" in your keyboard. This will skip your cursor to the patron vicinity in the form.

7.   Jump to the Amount Field: To jump to the amount area in a shape, press "Ctrl+Alt+A" on your keyboard. This will circulate your cursor to the amount area inside the shape.

Searching for Transactions

1.   Open the Search Bar: To open the quest bar, press "Ctrl+F" in your keyboard. This will open the hunt bar on the pinnacle of the net page.

2.   Search for a Transaction: To look for a transaction, kind the transaction's name, variety, or one of a kind identifying statistics

into the quest bar and press "Enter" on your keyboard. This will bring up a list of transactions that wholesome your are looking for requirements.

3.   Clear the Search Results: To smooth the hunt outcomes and flow decrease again to the general list of transactions, press "Esc" for your keyboard.

4.   Navigate the Search Results: To navigate the hunt effects, use the up and down arrow keys on your keyboard to highlight a transaction and press "Enter" to view its records.

5.   Filter the Search Results: To clean out the hunt effects, click at the "Filter" button within the are looking for bar or press "Ctrl+Alt+F" in your keyboard. This will deliver up a menu wherein you can choose out out filters which incorporates date range, transaction type, and extra.

6.   Save a Search: To save a search for destiny use, click on the "Save Search" button

within the are seeking out bar or press "Ctrl+Alt+Shift+F" for your keyboard. This will carry up a menu in which you may name and keep the search.

Editing Shortcuts

Basic Editing Shortcuts

1.   Cut Text: To cut determined on text, press "Ctrl+X" to your keyboard. This will do away with the selected textual content and keep it to the clipboard, permitting you to stick it a few other region.

2.   Copy Text: To reproduction determined on textual content, press "Ctrl+C" on your keyboard. This will preserve a duplicate of the selected textual content to the clipboard, allowing you to stick it some vicinity else.

three. Paste Text: To paste textual content from the clipboard, press "Ctrl+V" to your keyboard. This will insert the textual content from the clipboard at the present day cursor area.

4.   Undo Changes: To undo your ultimate movement, press "Ctrl+Z" on your keyboard. This will revert the file to the country it modified into in before the remaining motion have emerge as completed.

5.   Redo Changes: To redo an movement that changed into undone, press "Ctrl+Y" in your keyboard. This will repair the file to the state it modified into in before the undo movement have become completed.

6.   Select All: To pick out all textual content or records in a report, press "Ctrl+A" for your keyboard. This will spotlight all textual content or data in the record.

7.   Find and Replace: To find out specific text or facts in a file and update it with something else, press "Ctrl+H" to your keyboard. This will deliver up the discover and update verbal exchange field wherein you may input the text or statistics you want to find out and what you need to update it with.

Advanced Editing Shortcuts

1.	Move to Next Field: To float to the following problem at the same time as modifying a transaction or other information, press "Tab" to your keyboard. This will flow the cursor to the subsequent place inside the form or file.

2.	Move to Previous Field: To drift to the preceding vicinity while improving a transaction or different records, press "Shift+Tab" on your keyboard. This will circulate the cursor to the previous concern within the form or record.

3.	Add a New Line: To upload a new line at the identical time as improving a transaction or different statistics, press "Ctrl+Alt+Y" in your keyboard. This will upload a brand new line to the shape or record, permitting you to go into more information.

4.	Delete a Line: To delete a line at the same time as enhancing a transaction or excellent records, press "Ctrl+Alt+D" for your keyboard. This will delete the selected line from the shape or file.

5. Insert Today's Date: To insert extraordinarily-modern date whilst improving a transaction or exclusive records, press "Ctrl+; " in your keyboard. This will insert cutting-edge date on the modern cursor place.

6. Insert Current Time: To insert the cutting-edge-day time while improving a transaction or different records, press "Ctrl+Shift+:" for your keyboard. This will insert the modern time at the modern-day cursor place.

7. Auto-fill a Field: To automobile-fill a subject even as editing a transaction or one of a kind records, press "Ctrl+Down Arrow" for your keyboard. This will show a list of previously entered values for the chosen trouble, allowing you to pick out one and car-fill the sector.

Editing List Items

1. Navigate Between List Items: To navigate amongst list items, use the up and

down arrow keys for your keyboard. This will will let you fast go together with the glide among listing gadgets in a specific listing.

2.   Edit a List Item: To edit a listing item, pick out the object and press "Ctrl+E" for your keyboard. This will open the edit window for the selected listing object, allowing you to make changes to its facts.

3.   Copy a List Item: To replica a list item, choose the item and press "Ctrl+Alt+C" on your keyboard. This will create a reproduction of the chosen list object, permitting you to make adjustments to the replica while leaving the best object unchanged.

four.   Delete a List Item: To delete a listing object, select out the object and press "Ctrl+D" in your keyboard. This will delete the selected list object from the listing.

5.   Add a New List Item: To upload a brand new list object, press "Ctrl+N" on your keyboard. This will open the create a cutting-

edge window, in which you could enter the statistics for the brand new list object.

6. Move Between Fields: To circulate amongst fields even as editing a listing item, use the "Tab" key for your keyboard. This will will let you brief drift between fields and enter records for each region.

7. Save Changes: To preserve changes to a list object, press "Ctrl+S" to your keyboard. This will shop any modifications you made to the list object.

Chapter 3: Reporting Shortcuts

Generating Reports

1.   Open Reports: To open the evaluations menu, press "Ctrl+R" on your keyboard. This will open the reviews menu, in which you can select out the document you want to generate.

2.   Navigate Reports: To navigate through the reviews menu, use the up and down arrow keys on your keyboard. This will allow you to brief flow through the reviews and select the best you want to generate.

three. Run a Report: To run a record, select the record and press "Enter" to your keyboard. This will generate the record and show it on the show display.

four. Customize a Report: To customize a report, choose out the file and press "Ctrl+Alt+R" on your keyboard. This will open the custom designed record window, in which you can pick out out the alternatives and necessities for the document.

five.   Save a Report: To keep a file, press "Ctrl+S" on your keyboard on the equal time because the record is open. This will store the report with the contemporary settings and criteria.

6.   Print a Report: To print a record, press "Ctrl+P" for your keyboard at the same time because the report is open. This will open the print dialog subject, wherein you can pick out the printer and print settings.

7.   Export a Report: To export a document, press "Ctrl+Alt+E" in your keyboard at the equal time due to the fact the report is open. This will open the export communique box, in which you could pick out the report layout and holiday spot for the file.

Memorized Transaction Shortcuts

Creating Memorized Transactions

1.   Create a New Memorized Transaction: To create a brand new memorized transaction, press "Ctrl+T" to your keyboard. This will open the "New Transaction" window,

wherein you may choose out the transaction type you need to memorize.

2.   Memorize a Transaction: To memorize a transaction, pick the transaction and press "Ctrl+M" in your keyboard. This will open the "Memorize Transaction" window, in which you can input the data and set the frequency of the habitual transaction.

three. Edit a Memorized Transaction: To edit a memorized transaction, choose the transaction and press "Ctrl+E" for your keyboard. This will open the "Edit Memorized Transaction" window, where you may modify the records and frequency of the ordinary transaction.

four. Delete a Memorized Transaction: To delete a memorized transaction, pick out the transaction and press "Ctrl+D" for your keyboard. This will delete the memorized transaction from the listing.

five.   List Memorized Transactions: To list memorized transactions, press "Ctrl+T" for your keyboard, then pick out out "Memorized Transactions" from the transaction kind list. This will show a list of all memorized transactions.

6.   Use a Memorized Transaction: To use a memorized transaction, press "Ctrl+T" in your keyboard, then choose the memorized transaction you want to use from the list. This will populate the transaction shape with the information of the memorized transaction.

Invoice Shortcuts

Creating Invoices

1.   Create a New Invoice: To create a cutting-edge invoice, press "Ctrl+Alt+I" on your keyboard. This will open the "Create Invoice" window, wherein you could pick out the client, upload services or products, and enter one-of-a-kind statistics of the invoice.

2.   Add a New Line Item: To upload a modern-day line item to the invoice, press "Ctrl+Alt+N" for your keyboard. This will upload a ultra-modern line object to the bill

wherein you can input the goods or services records.

three. Save and Close an Invoice: To keep and near an invoice, press "Ctrl+Alt+S" to your keyboard. This will hold the invoice and close to the window.

4. Save and New: To keep the contemporary-day bill and create a new one, press "Ctrl+Alt+M" to your keyboard. This will shop the cutting-edge invoice and open a state-of-the-art invoice window.

five. Email an Invoice: To e-mail an invoice to the patron, choose out out the invoice and press "Ctrl+Alt+E" for your keyboard. This will open the "Send Invoice" window wherein you could enter the customer's e-mail deal with and send the invoice.

6. Copy an Invoice: To copy an current bill, pick out out the bill and press "Ctrl+Alt+C" for your keyboard. This will create a modern bill with the same statistics as the selected invoice.

Editing Invoices

1.   Edit an Invoice: To edit an invoice, pick the invoice and press "Ctrl+E" to your keyboard. This will open the "Edit Invoice" window wherein you can make modifications to the invoice.

2.   Add a New Line Item: To add a modern-day line object to the bill, press "Ctrl+Alt+N" on your keyboard. This will upload a today's line item to the invoice in which you may input the goods or services statistics.

three. Delete a Line Item: To delete a line object from the bill, choose out the street item and press "Ctrl+D" in your keyboard.

four.   Save and Close an Invoice: To maintain and close to an invoice, press "Ctrl+S" to your keyboard. This will store the bill and near the window.

five.   Save and New: To save the modern-day bill and create a contemporary one, press "Ctrl+Alt+M" on your keyboard. This will maintain the modern-day invoice and open a modern-day invoice window.

6.   Email an Invoice: To email an invoice to the customer, pick the bill and press "Ctrl+E" in your keyboard. This will open the "Edit Invoice" window wherein you may make modifications to the bill earlier than sending it.

List Shortcuts

Creating and Editing Lists

1.   Create a New List Item: To create a brand new list item, press "Ctrl+N" on your keyboard. This will open a new window wherein you can enter the statistics for the modern day listing item.

2.   Edit a List Item: To edit an modern listing item, select the object and press "Ctrl+E" in your keyboard. This will open the "Edit" window in which you could make modifications to the data of the list item.

3. Delete a List Item: To delete a list item, choose the object and press "Ctrl+D" for your keyboard. This will delete the chosen item from the list.

4. Copy a List Item: To reproduction a listing item, choose the item and press "Ctrl+C" in your keyboard. This will create a duplicate of the selected item.

5. Paste a List Item: To paste a list object, choose out the vicinity in that you need to stick the copied object and press "Ctrl+V" in your keyboard. This will paste the copied item to the selected vicinity.

6. Search for a List Item: To search for a list object, press "Ctrl+F" to your keyboard. This will open the hunt bar in which you could input the decision or records of the object you are seeking out.

Navigating and Sorting Lists

1. Move Between Fields: To pass among fields in a listing, use the "Tab" key to

transport to the following subject, or "Shift+Tab" to move to the previous region.

2.   Move Up or Down the List: To skip up or down the listing, use the "Up Arrow" key to transport up one row, or the "Down Arrow" key to move down one row.

three. Move to the Top or Bottom of the List: To flow into to the pinnacle of the list, press "Ctrl+Home" on your keyboard. To circulate to the bottom of the listing, press "Ctrl+End" in your keyboard.

four.   Sort the List: To kind the listing, click on at the column header you want to type thru. Click as quickly as to kind in ascending order or click times to type in descending order.

five.   Search for an Item: To look for an object inside the list, press "Ctrl+F" to your keyboard. This will open the search bar in which you may input the selection or facts of the object you are seeking out.

6.   Select Multiple Items: To choose multiple devices in the list, preserve down the

"Ctrl" key even as clicking at the devices you need to choose out out. To choose a number of objects, click on the number one object in the variety, maintain down the "Shift" key, and click on on the final item in the variety.

Search Shortcuts

Basic Search Shortcuts

1.   Quick Search: To perform a short seek in QuickBooks Online, click on on on at the magnifying glass icon within the pinnacle proper-hand nook of the show show display or press "Ctrl+F" to your keyboard. This will open the Quick Search bar, wherein you can input the call or facts of the item you are seeking out.

2.   Advanced Search: To perform a complicated are searching out, click on at the "Advanced" hyperlink next to the Quick Search bar. This will open the Advanced Search window, in which you may clean out your are in search of via unique standards,

together with date, form of transaction, or quantity.

3.   Clear Search: To easy your are seeking effects and start a brand new search, click on at the "X" icon next to the search bar or press "Esc" in your keyboard.

four.   Search Within a List: To are looking for within a list, together with a patron or supplier list, use the "Ctrl+F" keyboard shortcut to open the Quick Search bar. As you type inside the are in search of bar, the list will mechanically clean out to expose gadgets that during shape your attempting to find standards.

five.   Search Using Filters: To seek the use of filters, click on on on the "Filter" button on the top of a listing. This will open the Filter window, in which you can specify attempting to find requirements by the usage of using fields along with call, date, or amount.

Advanced Search Shortcuts

1.   Search thru the use of Transaction Type: To look for a specific shape of transaction, which incorporates invoices or payments, use the drop-down menu inside the Advanced Search window. Select the transaction type you need to look for and QuickBooks Online will filter your are looking for effects to great display that transaction type.

2.   Search by manner of way of Amount: To look for transactions that suit a particular dollar amount, input the quantity in the "Amount" place in the Advanced Search window. You can use the symbols "<" and ">" to look for transactions which are lots lots less than or greater than a fine quantity.

three. Search through Date: To look for transactions interior a particular date range, use the "From" and "To" date fields within the Advanced Search window. You also can use the drop-down menu to choose out a pre-described date variety, collectively with "Last Month" or "This Fiscal Year."

four. Search with the beneficial useful resource of Customer or Vendor: To look for transactions related to a specific customer or vendor, input the decision of the customer or seller inside the "Name" region within the Advanced Search window. QuickBooks Online will easy out your searching for results to awesome show transactions associated with that customer or provider.

five. Search through Memo or Description: To search for transactions based on a specific memo or description, input the textual content you need to look for in the "Memo/Description" vicinity in the Advanced Search window. QuickBooks Online will smooth out your seek outcomes to handiest show transactions that encompass that text within the memo or description area.

Chapter 4: Window Shortcuts

Basic Window Shortcuts

1.   Minimize Window: To reduce the cutting-edge window, press the Windows key + Down arrow key.

2.   Maximize Window: To maximize the modern-day-day window, press the Windows key + Up arrow key.

three. Switch Between Open Windows: To switch between open windows, press Alt + Tab. Keep urgent Tab while maintaining down the Alt key to cycle via all open domestic home windows.

four. Close Current Window: To near the contemporary window, press the Alt + F4 keys.

five.   Open Start Menu: To open the Start menu, press the Windows key.

6.   Open Task Manager: To open the Task Manager, press Ctrl + Shift + Esc.

7.   Lock Your Computer: To lock your laptop, press the Windows key + L.

8.   Take a Screenshot: To take a screenshot of the present day window, press Alt + Print Screen. To take a screenshot of the entire display show display screen, press the Windows key + Print Screen.

These number one window shortcuts will let you navigate and control domestic domestic home windows greater efficaciously on the same time as using QuickBooks Online. By using those shortcuts, you can preserve time and streamline your workflow.

Advanced Window Shortcuts

1.   Split Screen: To break up the present day window into panes, press the Windows key + Left arrow or Right arrow. This is beneficial whilst you need to paintings on two home windows on the identical time.

2.   Snap Windows: To snap a window to as a minimum one aspect of the show, drag it to the left or proper edge of the show display.

The window will robotically snap to fill 1/2 of the display display screen. This is beneficial while you want to assess two home home windows side via side.

3.   Task View: To open the Task View, press the Windows key + Tab. This permits you to view all open domestic home windows and transfer amongst them.

4.   Virtual Desktops: To create a modern day digital computer, press the Windows key + Ctrl + D. To transfer among virtual computer systems, press the Windows key + Ctrl + Left arrow or Right arrow.

5.   Shake Window: To restriction all particular open home home windows except the cutting-edge one, click on and keep the call bar of the modern-day window and shake it backward and forward.

6.   Close All Windows: To close all open domestic home windows, press the Windows key + Ctrl + F4.

By the use of those advanced window shortcuts, you can art work extra efficiently and manipulate more than one home windows more without problems at the equal time as the use of QuickBooks Online. These shortcuts allow you to preserve time and streamline your workflow, specifically in case you frequently need to paintings on a couple of windows or transfer amongst digital computer systems.

How to reset all shortcut modifications to default

To reset all keyboard shortcut adjustments to the default settings in QuickBooks Online, you could have a look at the ones steps:

1.   Log in to your QuickBooks Online account the use of your credentials.

2.   Once you are in the dashboard, click on on on the "Gear" icon located inside the pinnacle proper corner. This will open the QuickBooks Online settings.

three. From the drop-down menu that looks, pick out out "Keyboard shortcuts." This will open the Keyboard Shortcuts settings web page.

four. On the Keyboard Shortcuts settings internet net page, you may see a listing of all of the keyboard shortcuts and their assigned moves.

five. To reset all the keyboard shortcuts to their default settings, click on on on at the "Reset All" button. This will revert all the adjustments you made to the default settings.

6. A confirmation activate will seem asking if you need to reset all the shortcuts. Click on "Yes" to proceed.

7. Once you confirm the reset, all of the keyboard shortcuts may be restored to their particular default settings.

Please be aware that the particular steps and alternatives may additionally moreover range slightly relying on the model and format of QuickBooks Online you are the usage of. If you stumble upon any troubles or the options referred to above aren't to be had, I propose regarding the QuickBooks Online Help Center or contacting QuickBooks Online resource for further help.

Tips and Tricks

Open Multiple Browser Windows

When running with QuickBooks Online, using severa home windows right now is an remarkable time-saving strategy as it lets in you to without difficulty switch a number of the severa indicates. Comparisons among specific QuickBooks competencies or opinions also can be made speedy and outcomes the usage of this technique. You will want to hit the Refresh button on your browser for the modifications to emerge as visible.

By right-clicking the tab you are walking on to your browser and selecting the Duplicate desire, you may make it simply so the equal company record can be opened in severa browser home domestic home windows on the identical time. To make a reproduction of your contemporary tab in Internet Explorer, press the Control key and the letter K concurrently.

Now that you have two tabs hooked into your account, you have were given the choice of dragging one out of the window so you may go on outstanding monitors factor-through way of-difficulty. This is possible due to the fact you presently have tabs logged in to your account.

You can most effective use this smooth approach of starting a couple of tabs if every tab is viewing the equal agency. For viewing excellent businesses simultaneously, you've got got had been given options: incognito mode (or personal surfing) or more than one browsers.

Connect Your Bank & Credit Card Accounts

One of the maximum useful and green components of QuickBooks Online is a function referred to as on-line banking, it's occasionally known as monetary institution feeds. When you hyperlink an account, QuickBooks will down load and classify your financial institution and credit card transactions for you routinely; all you need to do is provide very last approval for the paintings that has been accomplished. You can link whichever many bills you word essential.

Click the Link Account button at the Banking internet net web page of QuickBooks Online, upload your account, after which observe the steps that seem at the show display to link your account records. This will assist you to be a part of your economic organization transactions and credit score score card debts.

Set Up Items for Every Product or Service You Provide

Products and services are the two primary training of commodities that may be sold using QuickBooks Online. It is highly recommended which you create devices for every products or services that you promote just so recording purchases and sending invoices may be finished a whole lot greater brief. Additionally, this may offer you with more depth inner critiques, allowing you to expose monetary facts in step with the product or service in query.

When you create a contemporary object, you will have the choice of selecting from four different sorts: stock, carrier, bundle, or non-stock. Bundles and stock tracking are skills which can be special to the Plus and Advanced stages of QuickBooks Online. The Bundle feature of Shopify allows you to package deal and sell severa objects as a unmarried product or service, while the Inventory feature of Shopify permits you to hold tabs at the first-class quantities and prices of merchandise in inventory.

Use the Undeposited Funds Account When Making a Deposit

In QuickBooks, a file of payments is maintained within the Undeposited Funds account till the ones bills are deposited inside the corresponding monetary organisation account. The cash and cheques which you deposit are often dealt with as part of a unmarried transaction thru maximum banks. When you have your deposit slip in hand and are aware of which payments your monetary institution has bundled together, you may be able to replicate this way in QuickBooks. This makes it an awful lot less complicated to examine the deposits recorded on your account join up in QuickBooks to the corresponding economic institution statements.

You may think of the Undeposited Funds account as a virtual "lockbox" that you positioned your payments in until you're prepared to take them to the monetary institution. This "lockbox" stores your cash till you're ready to take it to the economic company.

Chapter 5: Attachment Source Documents

Attachments may be uploaded and stored to every transaction in QuickBooks Online, which offers you greater flexibility. The way of referencing supply files is simplified and expedited because of this. Follow the steps underneath to characteristic an attachment in your message:

Step 1: Open an invoice or specific transaction.

Step 2: Click the Attachments icon inside the backside left nook.

Step 3: Browse for the documents you want to attach.

Step four: Click Save.

Set Up Recurring Transactions

You can preserve time through using automating the way of getting into character transactions that upward thrust up often with the beneficial aid of putting in regular transactions. This will let you enter transactions on the same time as now not having to manually enter every one in my opinion. These encompass bills for rent and payments, profits, and buy orders placed with various companies. It no longer best allows you hold time, but it additionally acts as a reminder for coming close to financial transactions.

Both the Essentials and editions of QuickBooks Online aid habitual transactions, and the method for growing them is as follows:

Step 1: Select the Gear icon on the top right of the display.

Step 2: Under Lists, choose out Recurring Transactions.

Step 3: Click New.

Step 4: Select the form of transaction to create and pick out OK.

Step five: Enter a template call.

Step 6: Choose a kind, which embody scheduled, unscheduled, or reminder.

Step 7: Enter the critical facts.

Step eight: Save the template.

At the very bottom of the invoice window is a button labeled "Make Recurring," which you may use to provoke the arrival of regular invoices.

Pay Bills Online Directly from QuickBooks

If you want to pay your bills on line, you do not need to download greater software program software due to the fact you can pay them at once indoors QuickBooks at the same time as no longer having to go out this gadget. You can effortlessly pay bills and ship tests to groups whilst you operate Online Bill Pay since it permits you to perform that without requiring the vendors to set up anything on their end.

It allows you to pay a invoice the use of a credit score card, after which QuickBooks

Online will write a take a look at and supply it to the seller for your behalf. In addition to this, you can pay invoices, make bill bills in real-time, and pay 1099 contractors the use of physical checks and financial group transfers.

Before you could employ Online Bill Pay, you could first must spark off it from inner your QuickBooks Online account. To try this:

Step 1: Click on +New.

Step 2: Select Pay Bills Online.

Step 3: Set up your monetary group account facts.

Step 4: Follow the activates to connect your monetary group account then maintain your adjustments.

Connect to Live Bank Feeds

If you be a part of the financial company account which you use for your corporation to QuickBooks Online, this system will preserve track of your account balances and transactions routinely. You won't need to worry approximately manually importing or coming into any facts. Since QuickBooks is properly matched with over 20,000 domestic and remote places banks, placing it up want to no longer provide an excessive amount of of a project.

To get started, go to the Banking tab after which select out one of the alternatives under the Link Accounts heading. To maintain with the synchronizing of your account, honestly take a look at the on-display screen instructions.

Transactions are updated mechanically once in line with day at night time time, but you furthermore may have the selection to replace manually on every occasion essential with truely one click on on.

QuickBooks Desktop Pro

1.   Invoicing: Businesses can produce and distribute consumer invoices professionally with QuickBooks Desktop Pro. The invoices

may be changed to embody your commercial employer's logo, fee conditions, and extraordinary data. You can screen the development of invoices and remind clients to make bills the usage of this tool.

2.   Expense tracking: By connecting their financial institution debts, credit score score playing playing cards, and unique economic money owed to this tool, groups can absolutely manage their spending the use of QuickBooks Desktop Pro. You can also classify your prices, embody receipts, and keep a watch for your cash go along with the float in actual-time.

three. Inventory control: QuickBooks Desktop Pro moreover offers solutions for handling inventories for agencies. You can installation reorder points, test stock levels, and make purchase orders. You also can create inventory evaluations the usage of this tool and hold tabs on inventory charges.

four. Payroll: Businesses may additionally moreover control their worker payroll using the payroll device in QuickBooks Desktop Pro. Payroll calculations, tax withholding, and tax form introduction are all viable. The software moreover gives payroll tax e-submitting and direct charge.

five. Financial reporting: Some economic evaluations produced through QuickBooks Desktop Pro help corporations in records their economic state of affairs. You can also moreover moreover produce reviews that provide you with records about the financial fitness of your employer employer, together with balance sheets, profits statements, cash go with the drift statements, and others.

Comprehensive accounting software program application like QuickBooks Desktop Pro can assist corporations in efficaciously managing their monetary operations. Automating repetitive operations and giving beneficial insights into a enterprise's monetary reputation, is a robust tool that can maintain businesses effort and time.

General Keyboard Shortcuts

Creating New Transactions

Creating new transactions is a common task completed in QuickBooks Desktop, and it can be done rapid and efficaciously the usage of keyboard shortcuts. Here are a number of the keyboard shortcuts for developing new transactions in QuickBooks Desktop:

1.   To create a new bill: Ctrl + I

2.   To create a cutting-edge income receipt: Ctrl + R

3.   To create a new credit memo: Ctrl + M

4.   To create a extremely-current purchase order: Ctrl + T

5.   To create a latest bill: Ctrl + B

6.   To create a current test: Ctrl + W

7.   To create a new estimate: Ctrl + E

8.   To create a new profits order: Ctrl + J

nine. To create a contemporary assertion: Ctrl + S

These keyboard shortcuts allow clients to create new transactions speedy and effectively, at the same time as not having to navigate thru menus and submenus. By using the ones shortcuts, customers can maintain time and increase their productivity whilst the usage of QuickBooks Desktop.

Editing Transactions

1.   To open the Edit Transaction window: Ctrl + E

2.   To delete a transaction: Ctrl + D

3.   To void a transaction: Ctrl + V

4.   To memorize a transaction: Ctrl + M

5.   To replica a transaction: Ctrl + O

6.   To paste a copied transaction: Ctrl + Y

7.   To clean a transaction: Ctrl + Delete

eight. To zoom in on a transaction: Ctrl + Alt + Z

9.   To connect a document to a transaction: Ctrl + Att

Deleting Transactions

1.   To delete a transaction: Ctrl + D

2.   To undo the final motion: Ctrl + Z

three. To void a transaction: Ctrl + V

4.   To delete more than one transactions without delay: Ctrl + Alt + D

Using the ones keyboard shortcuts, customers can quick and efficiently delete transactions in QuickBooks Desktop. The Ctrl + D shortcut is in particular beneficial while deleting a single transaction, on the same time because the Ctrl + Alt + D shortcut can be used to delete a couple of transactions right now. It is important to word that deleting transactions may want to have large consequences, and customers have to exercise caution at the identical time as using these shortcuts. It is continuously an splendid concept to make a backup of the QuickBooks report in advance than making any massive changes to the statistics.

Saving Transactions

1.   To hold a transaction: Ctrl + S

2.   To keep and new: Ctrl + Alt + S

three. To shop and close to: Ctrl + Enter

four.   To store and new consumer or vendor: Ctrl + Alt + N

five.   To keep and subsequent: Ctrl + Shift + S

Using those keyboard shortcuts, clients can preserve transactions rapid and correctly, without having to navigate through menus and submenus. The Ctrl + S shortcut is particularly beneficial whilst saving a transaction, while the Ctrl + Alt + S shortcut can be used to keep and create a modern-day transaction at the same time. The Ctrl + Enter shortcut can be used to store and close to a transaction, at the equal time because the Ctrl + Alt + N shortcut may be used to maintain and create a trendy patron or dealer. Finally, the Ctrl + Shift + S shortcut can be used to maintain and circulate to the following transaction inside the listing.

Copying and Pasting Transactions

1.   To reproduction a transaction: Ctrl + O

2.   To paste a copied transaction: Ctrl + Y

3.   To paste and upload new: Ctrl + Alt + Y

Using these keyboard shortcuts, clients can quick and without trouble reproduction and paste transactions into QuickBooks Desktop. The Ctrl + O shortcut is especially useful while copying a transaction, at the same time as the Ctrl + Y shortcut may be used to paste a copied transaction. The Ctrl + Alt + Y shortcut may be used to stick a copied transaction and upload a modern-day one on the equal time.

Chapter 6: Searching For Transactions

1.   Open the Search window:

Ctrl + F: Open the Search window.

2.   Navigate the hunt outcomes:

Up and Down arrow keys: Move up or down inside the searching for results.

Enter key: Select a transaction in the are attempting to find effects.

3.   Edit the selected transaction:

Ctrl + E: Edit the selected transaction.

four.   Delete the chosen transaction:

Ctrl + D: Delete the selected transaction.

5.   Create a contemporary transaction from the hunt window:

Ctrl + N: Create a present day transaction based totally totally mostly on the selected transaction.

Editing Shortcuts

Basic Editing Shortcuts

1.   Copy and Paste:

Ctrl + C: Copy determined on text or facts.

Ctrl + V: Paste copied text or facts.

2.   Undo and Redo:

Ctrl + Z: Undo the final movement.

Ctrl + Y: Redo the remaining undone motion.

3.   Cut and Paste:

Ctrl + X: Cut decided on textual content or records.

Ctrl + V: Paste lessen text or information.

4.   Selecting Text:

Shift + Arrow keys: Select textual content in the route of the arrow keys.

Ctrl + A: Select all textual content in a subject or record.

5.   Moving Text:

Cut the text the usage of Ctrl + X, circulate to the new vicinity, and paste the text the usage of Ctrl + V.

Advanced Editing Shortcuts

1.   Find and Replace:

Ctrl + F: Open the Find window to look for text or statistics.

Ctrl + H: Open the Replace window to update text or information.

2.   Navigate between phrases and lines:

Ctrl + Left or Right Arrow: Move the cursor one phrase to the left or proper.

Ctrl + Up or Down Arrow: Move the cursor one paragraph up or down.

3.   Selecting Blocks of Text:

Shift + Ctrl + Arrow keys: Select textual content in the course of the arrow keys through blocks.

Shift + Ctrl + Home: Select all textual content from the cursor position to the begin of the cutting-edge line.

Shift + Ctrl + End: Select all text from the cursor characteristic to the prevent of the cutting-edge line.

four.   Indenting Text:

Ctrl + M: Indent decided on text one tab prevent to the right.

Shift + Ctrl + M: Remove one tab save you of indentation from determined on text.

5.   Formatting Text:

Ctrl + B: Bold decided on text.

Ctrl + I: Italicize decided on textual content.

Ctrl + U: Underline decided on text.

Editing List Items

1.   Open the List window:

Ctrl + L: Open the List window.

2.   Edit the chosen listing item:

Ctrl + E: Edit the selected listing object.

3.   Delete the chosen list item:

Ctrl + D: Delete the chosen listing object.

four.   Create a new list item:

Ctrl + N: Create a brand new list object.

5.   Move the chosen list object up or down:

Alt + Up arrow key: Move the selected listing object up.

Alt + Down arrow key: Move the selected list object down.

6.   Indent or outdent a sub-object in a listing:

Tab key: Indent the selected sub-item to the right.

Shift + Tab: Outdent the selected sub-item to the left.

Reporting Shortcuts

Generating Reports

One of the maximum important abilities of QuickBooks Desktop Pro is the functionality to generate critiques. With the subsequent shortcuts, you can generate reviews short and without trouble:

1.   Open the Report Center: Ctrl + R

The Report Center is the precept hub for generating opinions in QuickBooks Desktop Pro. With this shortcut, you can speedy open the Report Center and get admission to a large form of pre-constructed opinions.

2.   Select a document: Up and Down arrow keys, Enter key

Once you have got opened the Report Center, you could use the arrow keys to navigate via the list of to be had evaluations. Pressing the Enter key will pick the highlighted report.

3.   Customize a record: Ctrl + H

To customize a file, you can use the Modify Report window. With this shortcut, you can rapid open the Modify Report window and make changes to the selected file.

four.   Display the document in a one in each of a kind layout: Ctrl + E

QuickBooks Desktop Pro allows you to expose opinions in masses of codecs, collectively with graphs and charts. With this shortcut, you can speedy transfer among special formats to find the only that works first-rate to your dreams.

five.   Print or Export a record: Ctrl + P, Ctrl + O

Once you have got generated a record, you can want to print it or export it to a report. With the ones shortcuts, you can short perform these responsibilities at the same time as now not having to navigate through a couple of menus.

Modifying Reports

In addition to producing evaluations, QuickBooks Desktop Pro allows you to alter critiques to higher suit your desires. With the following shortcuts, you can make changes to reviews quick and without problems:

1.   Add or put off columns: Ctrl + Alt + D

With the Display Columns window, you could upload or eliminate columns from a record to attention at the information that is most critical to you. With this shortcut, you could fast open the Display Columns window and make adjustments to the selected record.

2.   Move or resize columns: Ctrl + Alt + Left or Right arrow keys, Ctrl + Alt + Up or Down arrow keys

In addition to which includes or removing columns, you could also skip or resize columns to higher set up the statistics in a record. With the ones shortcuts, you can rapid flow into or resize columns whilst not having to use the mouse.

three. Change font and colour settings: Ctrl + T

To make a record greater visually appealing, you could exchange the font and shade settings. With this shortcut, you may fast open the Formatting tab inside the Modify Report window and make adjustments to the font and colour settings.

four. Save or memorize a custom designed file: Ctrl + M, Ctrl + S

If you've got got made modifications to a report which you want to apply once more inside the future, you may hold or memorize the custom designed record. With the ones shortcuts, you could fast store or memorize a document while now not having to navigate thru more than one menus.

Memorized Transaction Shortcuts

Creating Memorized Transactions

QuickBooks Desktop Pro gives severa shortcut keys to create a memorized transaction rapid. Here are the stairs to use the shortcut keys:

1.   Open QuickBooks Desktop Pro and go to the transaction you need to memorize, including an bill or invoice.

2.   Enter all of the data for the transaction, together with the patron or supplier facts, account information, and every other relevant records.

3.   Once you've got got entered all the info, press "Ctrl+M" on your keyboard.

four. In the "Memorize Transaction" window, input a name for the memorized transaction and pick the right alternatives for the way frequently you need the transaction to recur.

Chapter 7: Editing Invoices

1.   To edit an gift invoice: Ctrl + E

2.   To delete an invoice: Ctrl + D

3.   To replica an bill: Ctrl + Alt + D

List Shortcuts

Creating and Editing Lists

Here are the keyboard shortcuts for developing and enhancing lists in QuickBooks Desktop Pro:

1.   To open the Lists menu: Ctrl + L

2.   To create a modern listing object: Ctrl + N

3.   To edit an modern-day listing item: Ctrl + E

four.   To delete a list item: Ctrl + D

five.   To reproduction a list object: Ctrl + Alt + D

Navigating and Sorting Lists

Here are a few keyboard shortcuts for navigating and sorting lists in QuickBooks Desktop Pro:

1.   To glide up and down the list: Up arrow and Down arrow keys

2.   To flow into to the number one object at the listing: Home key

3.   To float to the closing item within the list: End key

4.   To skip to the subsequent page of the listing: Page Down key

five.   To skip to the preceding net page of the listing: Page Up key

6.   To type the listing with the useful resource of column: Click at the column header or use the Tab key to transport to the column header and press the Spacebar key to kind in ascending order, and then press once more to type in descending order.

Additionally, you may use the following shortcuts to speedy filter and search for items in the listing:

1.   To clear out the list: Ctrl + F

2.   To look for an item inside the list: Ctrl + F after which sort inside the are looking for key-word.

These shortcuts can be utilized in severa lists in QuickBooks Desktop Pro, such as the Chart of Accounts, Customers, Vendors, Items, and more.

Search Shortcuts

Basic Search Shortcuts

1.   To look for transactions: Ctrl + F or Ctrl + F3

2.   To look for customers, organizations, or employees: Ctrl + E

three. To look for an item: Ctrl + I

four.   To search for an account: Ctrl + A

5.   To search for a file: Ctrl + R

6.   To look for a assist mission depend: F1

These shortcuts will supply up the respective seek domestic home home windows for the gadgets you are searching out. From there, you may enter your are trying to find necessities and hit the Enter key to carry out the search.

Advanced Search Shortcuts

1.   To use superior searching for: Ctrl + Shift + F or Ctrl + Alt + F

2.   To keep a seek: Ctrl + Alt + S

3.   To edit a saved are seeking: Ctrl + Alt + E

4.   To delete a stored seek: Ctrl + Alt + D

The advanced are trying to find characteristic lets in you to create custom are trying to find requirements that could encompass more than one are looking for for terms, date levels, and additional. You can use this feature to search for specific transactions, clients, businesses, personnel, and particular items on your QuickBooks facts.

Here are some more shortcuts you could use to customise your searching for standards:

1.   To add a new seek term: Tab key

2.   To do away with a are searching for term: Backspace key

three. To trade the operator for a seek term: Spacebar key

Once you have were given created your search requirements, you may save it as a custom search for destiny use. You can also edit or delete saved searches as wished.

Window Shortcuts

Basic Window Shortcuts

1.   To decrease the active window: Windows key + Down arrow key or Alt + Spacebar, then N

2.   To maximize the energetic window: Windows key + Up arrow key or Alt + Spacebar, then X

3.   To restore the active window to its preceding length: Alt + Spacebar, then R

4.   To go together with the flow the energetic window: Alt + Spacebar, then M, then use the arrow keys to move the window to a modern-day function

5.   To near the energetic window: Alt + F4 or Ctrl + F4

6.   To switch among open home home windows: Alt + Tab or Windows key + Tab

These shortcuts may be used to manipulate the home home windows in QuickBooks Desktop Pro, permitting you to speedy lower, maximize, float, or near home windows as wanted. The Alt + Tab or Windows key + Tab shortcut can also be used to short transfer among open home windows without the usage of the mouse.

Advanced Window Shortcuts

1.   To split the active window: Ctrl + Alt + M

2.   To toggle the show of the menu bar: Ctrl + 1

3.   To toggle the display of the icon bar: Ctrl + 2

four.   To toggle the show of the reputation bar: Ctrl + 3

five.   To toggle the display of the toolbar: Ctrl + 4

These shortcuts permit you to customize the display of the QuickBooks Desktop Pro window, permitting you to reveal or conceal various elements which include the menu bar, icon bar, fame bar, and toolbar. The Ctrl + Alt + M shortcut may be used to break up the window, permitting you to view multiple areas of QuickBooks right now.

Resetting all keyboard shortcut changes to default

To reset all keyboard shortcut adjustments to their default settings in QuickBooks Desktop Pro, you can observe the ones steps:

1.   Open QuickBooks Desktop Pro to your laptop.

2.   Click on the "Edit" menu located on the top of the display.

3.   From the drop-down menu, choose "Preferences." This will open the Preferences window.

4.   In the Preferences window, click on on "General" at the left-hand element.

five.   Within the General options, click on on on on the "My Preferences" tab.

6.   Look for the "Shortcut" phase and click on the "Reset All" button. This will repair all keyboard shortcuts to their default settings.

7.   A confirmation spark off will appear asking in case you want to reset all the shortcuts. Click on "OK" to maintain.

8.   Once you confirm the reset, all the keyboard shortcuts can be reverted to their unique default settings.

Tips and Tricks

Customize the Icon Bar

When using QuickBooks Desktop Pro, the Icon Bar may be visible on the very pinnacle of the show. It has masses of icons that you could click on immediately to get get admission to to the capabilities which is probably maximum typically utilized. However, via default, it handiest shows a small desire of icons to choose from. Follow these commands in case you need to alter the Icon Bar with the aid of manner of which includes or removing icons:

Right-click on on on anywhere at the Icon Bar.

Click on Customize Icon Bar.

In the Customize Icon Bar window, you can upload or cast off icons via the use of choosing or deselecting the corresponding checkboxes.

You also can change the order of the icons with the resource of dragging and dropping them in the favored order.

Click on OK to store the changes.

Customizing the Icon Bar will can help you get entry to your often used capabilities more fast, improving your productiveness.

Customize Your Layout

You have the selection to tweak the layout of your QuickBooks Desktop software program software software, so that you can make it each more aesthetically fascinating and easier to manipulate. To try this, pick out Edit > Preferences > Desktop View from the menu bar.

You can replace QuickBooks to reveal one window or many home domestic home windows, exchange your coloration scheme, and update your preserve settings the usage of the My Preferences internet net page. You also can modify your coloration scheme proper right here. You can customise the talents which might be established at the Home internet internet web page via way of navigating to the Company Preferences tab.

Customize Reports

There are numerous critiques to be had in QuickBooks Desktop. You also can thank your lucky stars which you can no longer must spend time searching through all of the reviews to choose out those that you use most customarily. You can customise and store favored reviews, permitting you to get right of entry to the maximum important ones with only a single click on at any time.

To keep a document as a fave, go to Reports > Report Center, attempting to find through the available opinions, after which click on at the coronary coronary heart picture that appears underneath each one. The Favorite tab in the Report Center will now display each of the reports which have been marked for viewing.

You may also speedy examine your favorites with the aid of way of clicking the Run Favorite Reports button, it really is placed at the icon bar.

Customize the Quick Access Toolbar

The clean Access Toolbar is a place of the QuickBooks Desktop Pro window that may be observed inside the pinnacle-left corner. This place gives customers easy get admission to to moves that are used regularly. The toolbar is pre-populated with sure actions which might be frequently positioned to use, collectively with "Save," "Print," and "Email." Users, however, can personalize the toolbar via together with any new commands that they discover themselves using frequently.

You can customise the toolbar with the aid of proper-clicking on it and deciding on the Customize Quick Access Toolbar choice from the context menu. Users may be able to select out the commands that they want to function or delete from the toolbar from this vicinity.

Use the Memorized Transactions Feature

You can set up and absolutely automate normal monetary transactions, together with invoices, payments, and exams, with the help of the Memorized Transactions tool this is included in QuickBooks Desktop Pro. The following is a rundown at the way to make benefit of the Memorized Transactions characteristic:

1.   Construct the transaction which you want to research through coronary coronary heart.

2.   Navigate to the Edit menu and pick out out the Memorize [transaction type] opportunity.

three. In the field classified "Memorize Transaction," offer the transaction a name and pick out the big kind of times every day which you need it to be carried out.

four.   In addition, you have were given had been given the opportunity to choose severa alternatives, consisting of the day on which to go into the transaction, the amount of days earlier on which to go into it, and the kind of times on which to go into it.

5.   To preserve the transaction which you have remembered, click on on the OK button.

Once you have got set up a memorized transaction, QuickBooks Desktop Pro will routinely input the transaction for you on the specific frequency. This can prevent time and help you keep away from mistakes.

Use the Vendor and Customer Centers

Both the Vendor Center and the Customer Center are beneficial tools for coping with facts related to corporations and customers. Customers might also furthermore use the Customer Center to observe information which includes invoices, bills, and estimates, whilst Vendors can use the Customer Center to view records which include rate records, purchase orders, and payments. Choose the applicable center from the menu categorized

Customers or Vendors to enter the Vendor or Customer Center, respectively.

Set Up Automatic Invoicing

Users may also moreover benefit from time financial economic financial savings afforded through the automation offered thru automated invoicing, which streamlines the billing manner. Users may additionally additionally set up automated invoicing thru way of going to the clients menu, deciding on produce Invoices, deciding on the customers they need to bill, and then choosing the selection to Automatically produce invoices for routine charges. This will whole the tool.

Use the Cash Flow Projector

When it involves making correct projections of destiny coins waft, the Cash Flow Projector is a useful tool. Users can generate forecasts for a period of up to 6 months in advance with the aid of using the Cash Flow Projector. To use the Cash Flow Projector, visit the

Planning and Budgeting menu and pick Cash Flow Projector from the list of options.

Use the Audit Trail

Within QuickBooks Desktop Pro, each alteration that is made to a transaction is logged in the Audit Trail. Users can make use of the Audit Trail to research troubles or reveal the adjustments which have been made through wonderful customers. To get to the Audit Trail, go to the number one menu, click on on Reports, then pick out out Accountant and Taxes, and eventually, pick out Audit Trail from the drop-down menu that appears.

Chapter 8: Using the QuickBooks Interface

To effectively use QuickBooks' capabilities and automate your economic duties, you need to be capable of navigate the software software's character interface. Let's have a look at the principle QuickBooks interface additives and the way to apply them:

1. Dashboard: The QuickBooks dashboard acts as your maximum crucial hub and gives a summary of the financial reputation and crucial performance metrics of your employer employer. Explore the dashboard for a moment and become cushty with its abilties, which might comprise graphs, charts, account balances, and present day day interest. The dashboard gives insightful statistics at a glance, allowing you to assess the circumstance of your agency corporation effects.

2. Navigation Bar: The navigation bar, that is on the left aspect of the show, is your entryway to many QuickBooks sections and

abilities. It consists of menu gadgets or symbols that stand in for severa modules, such as those for clients, groups, banking, opinions, and further. You can undertake positive sports activities associated with such regions through journeying the sections with the aid of way of clicking on the corresponding icons in the amazing elements. Consider spending a while turning into familiar with the navigation bar and the modules it offers access to.

three. Company Snapshot: A sturdy characteristic that gives an extensive compare of your organisation's monetary scenario is the Company Snapshot. It compiles critical economic information and suggests it in an attention grabbing way. Go to the QuickBooks dashboard and pick the "Company Snapshot" tab to get the Company Snapshot. You also can discover key indicators, graphs, and charts that shed light in your corporation's achievement right proper right here. You may additionally additionally alter the Company

Snapshot to show simplest the data that is most pertinent on your requirements.

4. Home Screen: The shortcuts to common responsibilities and reminders are placed on the QuickBooks domestic display screen. The domestic show display screen may be altered to reflect your tastes and higher meet your requirements. To modify the house show, click on at the tools icon within the top-right nook of the display and then choose out "Customize Home Page." From there, you may determine which alternatives to reveal or cover, how they need to be organized, or maybe upload your shortcuts. You can extra short get right of entry to typically used capabilities with the resource of customizing the home display.

5. Search Bar: The QuickBooks software program software has a search bar that lets in you to without trouble discover precise transactions, reviews, or capabilities. The are searching out bar, this is positioned at the top of the show screen, is a useful device for

finding fantastic statistics at the identical time as not having to undergo severa menus. Simply type a time period or phrase that describes what you are trying to find, and QuickBooks will deliver effects that are pertinent to your seek.

You'll be able to float via this device with performance and effortlessly in case you're familiar with the dashboard, navigation bar, Company Snapshot, home display display display screen, and are seeking bar, that are all crucial additives of the QuickBooks person interface. Your capability to get right of get right of entry to to the equipment you require, automate your financial duties, and make the maximum of QuickBooks for inexperienced financial control may be boosted by means of using your familiarity with the software software program.

2.1 EXAMINING THE NAVIGATION BAR AND DASHBOARD

It's time to get acquainted with QuickBooks' consumer interface as quickly as you have correctly installed it. You may additionally moreover get entry to a whole lot of features and duties thru the usage of the dashboard and navigation bar, which can be critical additives. You need to understand the followings:

Dashboard: Your number one get admission to point for critical records and responsibilities is the QuickBooks dashboard. It offers a precis of the financial reputation of your corporation, similarly to information on unpaid bills, account balances, and state-of-the-art sports activities sports. Explore the dashboard's many additives for a minute to become comfortable with the insightful records it gives rapid.

Navigation Bar: The navigation bar, usually visible at the left element of the display, gives brief get proper of access to to QuickBooks' diverse sections and capabilities. It has severa symbols or menu alternatives that stand in for severa modules, which incorporates Customers, Vendors, Banking, Reports, and others. You might also moreover adventure to severa components and carry out unique movements associated with those locations through clicking on those icons.

2.2 MAKING HOME SCREEN MODIFICATIONS

You may additionally additionally modify QuickBooks' default domestic display to fit your tastes and the sports you do most frequently. You may additionally moreover additionally optimize your productivity and effects get entry to regularly used capabilities with the resource of customizing the residence show. The home display display can be modified as seen proper right here:

On the top-right nook of the display show display, click on the system icon then pick out "Customize Home Page."

You can also additionally pick which capabilities to show or cover on your property show within the customization box. The order of the devices can also be modified through dragging and dropping them.

To keep time and growth productivity, think about growing shortcuts to commonly used evaluations or abilities.

When you've got completed customizing, click on "Done" to maintain your changes and move once more to the residence display show display.

2.Three   Comprehending   the   Business Snapshot

One of QuickBooks' maximum beneficial functions, the Company Snapshot, offers you an intensive summary of your organisation's economic state of affairs and overall performance. It compiles critical monetary statistics and offers it in an attention-grabbing manner. What you need to realize approximately the Company Snapshot is as follows:

Getting to the Company Snapshot: Go to the QuickBooks dashboard and click on on at the "Company Snapshot" choice to look the Company Snapshot. Additionally, you could get it thru the Reports menu with the aid of first selecting "Company & Financial" and then "Company Snapshot.

Important signs and symptoms and Charts: The Company Snapshot consists of big signs which incorporates income and spending traits, account balances, and income via the use of client or product. Additionally, it could have graphs or charts that graphically show the economic fulfillment of your business enterprise.

Personalizing the Company Snapshot: QuickBooks gives you the choice of personalizing the information showed within the Company Snapshot. You have the choice to choose the metrics and charts to reveal, alternate the order in which they appear, and outline the date levels for the furnished information.

Chapter 9: Setting up Your Company File

You need to set up your enterprise file, which acts as the basis to your economic data, to make use of QuickBooks in your enterprise efficiently. A new company corporation document must be created, alongside side the configuration of the chart of bills and key business enterprise settings. Let's test every movement in greater intensity:

3.1 MAKING A NEW COMPANY FILE

Setting your financial manage system starts offevolved with the resource of developing a current-day enterprise file in QuickBooks. Create a new commercial enterprise business enterprise record with the useful resource of following these steps:

Open QuickBooks and pick "New Company" from the File menu or click on on the "Create a contemporary day business enterprise" alternative.

Give the important facts, like business enterprise name, cope with, cellular telephone amount, area, and form of business business enterprise.

The accounting period on your economic sports sports is decided via the begin date of your financial yr, that you want to select.

Select the right tax form in your business enterprise's tax reporting desires.

According to the precise necessities of your corporation, QuickBooks will lead you via further activates to modify your agency report.

3.2 ADDING ORGANIZATION DATA AND PREFERENCES

Time to enter critical employer records and configure picks whilst the enterprise report has been created. What you need to do is as follows:

Company Information: Provide the contact records in your commercial business enterprise, which encompass its location, phone range, and net internet site on-line.

Your invoices, purchase orders, and extraordinary documents will include this records.

Financial Preferences: Set up monetary alternatives which consist of your own home distant places money, tax settings, and reporting foundation (coins or accrual). How QuickBooks manages monetary transactions and offers opinions will rely upon those options.

Sales and clients: Establish default fee conditions, income tax settings, and customer communique choices about earnings.

Purchases and Vendors: Set default rate terms, purchase tax settings, and dealer communication alternatives.

Setting up the Chart of Accounts: The chart of bills, which classifies and arranges your economic sports, is an important a part of your commercial enterprise organization record. The QuickBooks chart of debts can be set up as follows:

Recognize Different Account Kinds: Become acquainted with numerous account types, which include assets, liabilities, fairness, earnings, and fees. You can also efficiently categorize transactions with the usage of this information.

Add Accounts: Based at the financial necessities of your business employer, add debts to the chart of money owed. These may encompass credit score gambling playing playing cards, financial organization bills, money owed for income and prices, and further.

Account Names and Numbers Can Be Customized Create particular account names and numbers that correspond to the terminology or numbering scheme used by your enterprise.

Sub Accounts and Classes: If your economic reporting desires are complex, you have to think about which include sub-money owed or education to add greater depth and categorization in your chart of money owed.

For specific and powerful economic control, it's far important to spend time installing your enterprise commercial enterprise organization document in QuickBooks correctly. You construct a sturdy foundation for monitoring and dealing with your financial transactions by using manner of establishing a modern-day enterprise business enterprise document, which encompass corporation statistics and opportunities, and customizing the chart of payments. This ensures that QuickBooks efficaciously represents the monetary activity of your organisation and lets you produce insightful reviews and information for sound choice-making.

MANAGING SALES AND CUSTOMERS

Any organisation must effectively control patron information and income transactions. To help you in dealing with diverse components of your company efficiently, QuickBooks offers a whole lot of effective competencies. Let's test the vital moves had to control profits and customers in QuickBooks:

4.1 UPDATING AND ADDING CUSTOMER DATA

Follow the ones techniques to feature and amend consumer statistics in QuickBooks to preserve correct purchaser data:

Click at the Customers tab beneath the QuickBooks navigation bar and pick out "Customer Center."

Add a trendy customer, click the "New Customer & Job" button. Provide the touch statistics for the consumer, which incorporates name, cope with, telephone extensive range, and email.

Save the customer's records, and QuickBooks will provide a completely unique client ID for destiny use.

Find the consumer in the patron Center, double-click on on their call, make the favored changes, and keep the revisions to amend their data.

You can speedy get proper of entry to purchaser statistics at the equal time as making invoices, monitoring bills, and generating opinions through which includes and keeping updated consumer information.

four.2 ESTABLISHING AND BILLING CUSTOMERS

Fundamental to handling income in QuickBooks is developing and doling out invoices on your clients. To produce and ship invoices, adhere to the subsequent steps:

Select the "Create Invoice" alternative on the QuickBooks domestic internet page.

To upload a present day consumer, click on on on "Add New" or pick out the preferred customer from the drop-down menu.

The devices or services supplied, their quantities, fees, and any suitable discounts or profits tax need to be entered.

Make the bill template your personal thru placing your logo, changing the fashion, or incorporating special feedback.

Choose whether to print, email, or ship the bill using QuickBooks' incorporated messaging choice after saving it.

By sending customers their invoices on time, you could create easy price conditions, facilitate on-time bills, and enhance your coins float.

Refunds and Sales Receipt Management: In addition to handling invoices, QuickBooks moreover lets you keep music of sales receipts and technique refunds as wanted. How to deal with profits receipts and address refunds is as follows:

Sales Receipts: When acquiring set off price for services or products, profits receipts are carried out. A profits receipt can be created by means of using technique of selecting "Sales Receipt" from the QuickBooks home net web page, choosing the consumer, moving into the data of the object or company, and saving the receipt. This is beneficial for corporations who preference to file modern-day income transactions but do now not want to problem invoices.

Refunds: Go to the patron Center, find the customer, and pick out the "Refund" desire in case you need to offer a patron coins decrease again for back objects or canceled offerings. Process the refund thru following the on-show display screen instructions, ensuring that the right money owed are efficiently debited and credited.

QuickBooks' control of income receipts and refunds offers correct transaction documentation and allows correct financial reporting.

4.Three TRACKING CUSTOMER PAYMENTS

Monitoring Outstanding Balances, Account Reconciliation, and Maintaining Accurate Financial Records all Require Tracking Customer Payments. The following is the way to display screen consumer payments in QuickBooks:

Select the "Receive Payments" alternative at the QuickBooks home page.

From the drop-down menu, select out out the purchaser.

Enter the charge statistics, which include the amount, date, technique, and any applicable reference numbers.

Select the invoices to which the fee applies to use the price to the ones precise invoices.

When you keep the price, QuickBooks will reflect it in the consumer's stability.

You can hold tune of unpaid bills, speak with customers, and ensure that your debts receivable are current thru monitoring patron bills.

Chapter 10: Vendor and Expense Management

To keep accurate monetary records and successfully manage your enterprise's payables, coping with supplier records and costs is critical. The effective tool of QuickBooks make monitoring costs and coping with companies simple. Let's have a examine the crucial strategies in QuickBooks supplier and price management:

5.1 MANAGING AND ADDING VENDOR DATA

Follow these techniques to create and control provider data in QuickBooks to guarantee correct provider facts and smooth conversation:

Click the Vendors tab on the QuickBooks navigation bar, then click on on on "Vendor Center."

To add a modern dealer, click on at the "New Vendor" button. Provide contact statistics for the company, along facet call, cope with, cellular telephone variety, and electronic mail.

QuickBooks will assign a special provider ID at the identical time as you hold the vendor's records for future use.

In the Vendor Center, locate the vendor by means of the use of double-clicking on their name, make the correct changes, and then save the updates.

The capacity to rapid get right of access to fashionable-day dealer facts in QuickBooks makes it feasible to record bills, manage spending, and produce opinions.

five.2 BILL RECORDING AND PAYMENT

Accurate bill recording and price are critical for dealing with coins drift correctly and retaining amazing supplier people of the family. To input and pay bills in QuickBooks, comply with the ones steps:

Depending on whether or not or not you are getting into a modern invoice or paying an vintage one, pick "Enter Bills" or "Pay Bills" from the QuickBooks domestic show.

From the drop-down menu, pick out the seller, or click on "Add New" to feature a new provider.

Enter the bill's statistics, which includes the bill range, rate due date, famous, and any profits tax or reductions that could be relevant.

When paying bills, hold the bill and pick the proper charge method and date.

You might also moreover furthermore use direct financial institution transfers to pay payments electronically or print assessments using QuickBooks.

You can keep a comprehensive photo of your payables and guarantee on-time provider payments with the resource of effectively moving into and paying bills in QuickBooks.

five.Three TRACKING EXPENSES AND REIMBURSEMENTS:

Keeping music of prices and reimbursements is crucial for dealing with worker reimbursements and maintaining tabs on corporation spending. Here is the manner to apply QuickBooks to display costs and reimbursements:

Select "Expenses" or "Expense Transactions" from the QuickBooks home page.

Choose the right spending beauty, along facet utilities, adventure, or place of job resources.

Include the date, the charge amount, the vendor (if applicable), and any assisting paperwork.

If a fee is reimbursable, link it to the employee or corporation who incurred it.

For unique tracking, QuickBooks lets you partner spending with sure debts, collectively with monetary group payments or credit playing playing cards.

You might also additionally furthermore studies more about your enterprise employer's spending conduct, hold music of tax-deductible prices, and efficaciously deal with reimbursements by way of manner of keeping music of both expenses and reimbursements in QuickBooks.

5.4 MANAGING PURCHASE ORDERS:

Keeping tune of orders, ensuring correct stock management, and upholding strong dealer relationships all depend upon handling buy orders. How to manipulate purchase orders in QuickBooks is as follows:

Select "Create Purchase Orders" from the QuickBooks home internet internet page's menu.

From the drop-down menu, pick out out the vendor, or click on "Add New" to feature a new dealer.

Enter the products and portions you are ordering, collectively with the costs and any to be had reductions.

A buy order created thru QuickBooks may be emailed to the vendor for approval and processing.

You may also additionally moreover remodel the purchase order right right into a invoice or sales receipt at the same time as you get the devices or offerings to document the transaction.

Using QuickBooks to control purchase orders allows green dealer touch, precise inventory manage, and efficient procurement.

You also can optimize your payables and expenditure monitoring operations via efficaciously coping with agencies and charges in QuickBooks by using the use of adding and keeping issuer statistics, recording and paying bills, tracking costs and reimbursements, and managing purchase orders. With the help of QuickBooks' many talents, you can successfully manage supplier relationships, keep accurate monetary facts, and observe critical subjects approximately the fees and coins waft of your agency.

BANKING AND RECONCILIATION

Maintaining correct economic facts and protective the integrity of your monetary records embody coping with your monetary organization bills and reconciling your monetary statements. The robust features of QuickBooks make banking and reconciliation strategies easier. Let's examine the primary QuickBooks banking and reconciliation steps.

6.1 ESTABLISHING ONLINE BANKING AND OPENING BANK ACCOUNTS

Follow those techniques to set up your bank bills and connect to on line banking to effectively control your economic group bills in QuickBooks and streamline your economic transactions:

On the navigation bar of the QuickBooks domestic display display display, choose out the "Banking" button, then pick out out "Add Account."

You can also moreover either kind the name of the monetary organization or select it from the list of time-venerated economic institutions.

When caused, offer your economic organization login statistics to hyperlink QuickBooks for your on line banking.

QuickBooks can be part of securely in your economic group and import all of your financial institution transactions for you.

You may additionally accelerate the method of importing and classifying your financial institution transactions thru linking your economic business enterprise money owed to QuickBooks. This will cut down on manual information get admission to and preserve time.

6.2 RECORDING DEPOSITS AND WITHDRAWALS FROM THE BANK

For preserving correct monetary records, it's far important to efficaciously record economic institution deposits and withdrawals. To enter monetary group withdrawals and deposits into QuickBooks, study those steps:

From the QuickBooks domestic internet web page, choose the applicable monetary institution account through clicking the "Banking" tab within the navigation bar.

To file financial institution deposits, click on on the "Record Deposit" opportunity. Enter the deposit statistics, including the date, quantity, deliver, and any applicable customer or invoice data.

Click on "Write Checks" or "Pay Bills" to enter financial institution withdrawals. Enter the withdrawal facts, which embody the date, payee, sum, and any pertinent account or fee information.

Your economic information will wholesome up together together with your real monetary institution sports in case you efficaciously document financial group withdrawals and deposits in QuickBooks.

6.Three COMBINING CREDIT CARD AND BANK STATEMENTS

A essential step to making sure the extraordinary and integrity of your monetary information is to reconcile your monetary agency and credit score card statements with QuickBooks. To reconcile your financial institution and credit score card statements in QuickBooks, comply with these steps:

From the QuickBooks domestic show screen, choose the applicable economic organization account or credit rating card account through the usage of clicking the "Banking" tab in the navigation bar.

Select the announcement length you desire to reconcile with the useful resource of clicking the "Reconcile" alternative.

A economic group or credit card assertion and the transactions stated in QuickBooks want to be compared.

If the transactions healthful those to your statement, mark them as "Cleared" in QuickBooks.

Investigate and locate any faulty or lacking transactions to treatment any inconsistencies.

QuickBooks will display a reconciliation document detailing the correctness of your monetary statistics as soon as all transactions were reconciled.

By regularly reconciling your financial organization and credit score card statements in QuickBooks, you may make smarter financial selections due to the fact that your monetary facts will exactly constitute your actual financial activities.

6.4 HANDLING BANK DISCREPANCIES AND ERRORS

You may additionally want to every now and then run sooner or later of monetary organization inaccuracies or disparities whilst balancing your bills. You might also additionally correctly control these times with the aid of capabilities that QuickBooks offers. Here's a manner to deal with bank inconsistencies and issues in QuickBooks:

Review your monetary group statement and examine it for your QuickBooks transactions to find out the mismatch.

If you find out a economic institution mistake, get in touch in conjunction with your financial company to get the hassle steady and your economic corporation information up to date.

Investigate the transaction and join any mistakes or inconsistencies in case you discover a discrepancy that QuickBooks has made.

Make the desired adjustments in QuickBooks to as it need to be stability the payments.

You can also maintain the accuracy of your economic facts and guarantee the integrity of your economic facts through suddenly solving bank mistakes and inconsistencies in QuickBooks.

Chapter 11: Managing Inventory

For groups that cope with tangible matters, effective inventory manipulate is essential. You also can furthermore set up, display, and make changes to your inventory ranges and expenses with the aid of QuickBooks' many talents. Let's study the number one strategies for controlling inventory in QuickBooks:

7.1 ADDING ITEMS TO THE INVENTORY:

Follow those commands to installation your stock items in QuickBooks so you can control your stock correctly:

On the navigation bar of the QuickBooks domestic show, select out out the "Inventory" button, then pick out "Inventory Center."

Adding a present day day inventory item, click on the "New Item" button.

Provide records at the item, which include its name, description, SKU or factor range, earnings rate, and price.

List the bills for the object's related sales and prices.

Establish the initial inventory diploma for the item.

When you preserve the object, QuickBooks will supply it a totally unique item ID for destiny use.

You can efficiently manage your stock tiers, expenses, and income thru the use of growing inventory objects in QuickBooks.

7.2 MONITORING INVENTORY COSTS AND LEVELS

QuickBooks' inventory monitoring abilties make it much less hard to preserve a look ahead to your goods and gauge your profitability. To maintain tabs on inventory prices and levels, look at the ones steps:

On the navigation bar of the QuickBooks domestic display screen, select the "Inventory" button, then pick "Inventory Center."

View your cutting-edge inventory ranges, to be had stock quantities, and popular rate with the Inventory Center.

When you are making a sale, QuickBooks routinely modifies the inventory levels and makes use of the not unusual price method to determine the fee of gadgets furnished.

Review your inventory levels periodically to make sure they're accurate and make changes as wished, collectively with to account for broken or antique merchandise.

You can control your charges and profitability with the aid of using the usage of keeping track of stock tiers and charges in QuickBooks.

7.Three MODIFYING STOCK AND PRODUCING REPORTS ON STOCK

Maintaining correct data and acquiring insights into your inventory performance need you to behavior inventory reports and make changes for your stock ranges. To adjust stock and run inventory reviews, comply with the ones steps:

From the primary web web page of QuickBooks, pick the "Inventory" tab and then choose out "Adjust Quantity/Value on Hand."

To exchange the quantity of a given item reachable, use the adjustment alternative. Give a justification for the trade.

Make changes to account for missing or damaged items, refunds, or another inconsistencies in the inventory.

Run stock evaluations frequently to assess the charge, quantity, and earnings commonplace overall performance of your stock, which consist of the Inventory Valuation Summary or Inventory Stock Status.

You may also additionally maintain correct inventory statistics and gather know-how to make clever judgments approximately your products thru changing inventory stages as important and appearing inventory evaluations in QuickBooks.

You may also successfully control and optimize your stock by way of manner of putting in stock gadgets, tracking inventory ranges and charges, editing inventory as preferred, and on foot stock reviews the use of QuickBooks. With the beneficial aid of QuickBooks' brilliant competencies, you could optimize profitability by means of streamlining your inventory methods, keeping accurate data, and gaining useful insights into your inventory overall performance.

EMPLOYER MANAGEMENT AND PAYROLL

For businesses, dependable payroll, and employees records control is crucial. To simplify payroll techniques and guarantee payroll tax observance, QuickBooks offers a sizeable kind of system. Let's examine some important QuickBooks payroll and personnel control capabilities:

8.1 CONFIGURING PAYROLL PRÉFÉRENCES AND EMPLOYEE DATA

Follow these steps to efficiently manipulate worker repayment in QuickBooks:

Add Employee Information: Add employee facts to QuickBooks, which includes names, residences, Social Security numbers, and withholding records.

Define your alternatives for payroll: Set up your QuickBooks payroll choices, which incorporates pay durations, tax expenses, and deductions. Set your direct deposit opportunities, if crucial.

Track Sick and Vacation Time: Enter and screen worker ill and tour time in QuickBooks just so payroll charges may be calculated and recommended with accuracy.

You can simplify payroll techniques and assure right pay to your personnel by way of manner of installing worker statistics and payroll choices.

eight.2   PAYROLL   MANAGEMENT   AND PAYCHECK ISSUANCES

QuickBooks offers talents to make payroll management and paycheck issuance clean. Take those moves:

Track employee paintings hours or import time records from a time-tracking device thru getting into time records.

Compute Payroll: Using the employee's hourly charge, profits, or commission structure, QuickBooks computes the worker's pay. It takes into consideration every everyday and further time hours in addition to any unique compensation kinds, which include commissions or bonuses.

Review and Approve Payroll: Review the computed quantities for each worker and make any required corrections in advance than finishing payroll. Approve the payroll for processing after verification.

Issue Paychecks: Create employee paychecks, both as paper checks or thru direct deposit. Direct deposit payments can be crafted from inner QuickBooks or checks may be determined in the software.

You can simplify the way, reduce mistakes, and guarantee that your employees advantage timely and correct repayment by way of processing payroll and sending paychecks inner of QuickBooks.

8.Three MANAGING TAXES AND FORMS RELATED TO PAYROLL

An vital a part of dealing with employees is retaining tune of payroll taxes and office work. This manner is made less complicated by manner of QuickBooks' automatic abilties. Think approximately the following actions:

Calculate Payroll Taxes: Based on the employee's location and tax affiliation, QuickBooks computes federal and country payroll taxes mechanically. It takes into interest exemptions, deductions, and one-of-a-kind elements.

Payroll Tax Filings: QuickBooks produces payroll tax documents likke W-2s for employees and 1099s for impartial contractors. It aids to your endured compliance with tax jail tips and filing cut-off dates.

post Payroll Taxes: QuickBooks lets in you to on-line pay and publish payroll taxes, which is straightforward and guarantees activate price to the right tax businesses.

Using QuickBooks to govern payroll taxes and workplace work will expedite the way, restriction manual mistakes, and guarantee that each one tax felony pointers are positioned.

Businesses must efficaciously control worker reimbursement, which incorporates installing area worker statistics and payroll alternatives, processing payroll, dispensing paychecks, and coping with payroll taxes and office artwork. To streamline the ones methods, maintain time spent on them, and guarantee correct and prison payroll control, QuickBooks gives a whole lot of powerful tools and automation.

CREATING REPORTS AND ANALYSIS

Understanding your agency's financial popularity and making clever choices rely upon producing opinions and doing evaluation. You can also have a look at your financial information the usage of some of critiques and analytical gear provided with the useful aid of QuickBooks. Let's test the precept strategies for developing reviews and doing analyses in QuickBooks:

9.1 QUICKBOOKS REPORTS OVERVIEW

A massive variety of reports that QuickBooks gives offer useful insights into numerous components of your business enterprise's economic trendy overall performance. These opinions provide data on earnings, profitability, cash go with the flow, earnings and charges, and further. Following are some regularly used QuickBooks opinions:

Profit and Loss (Income Statement): Gives a pinnacle degree view of the sales, charges, and net income or loss for a given duration to your employer.

Balance Sheet: Provides a photograph of your employer's economic reputation thru presenting a picture of its belongings, liabilities, and fairness at a sure issue in time.

Cash Flow Statement: This file depicts the movement of coins into and from your organization and offers data about your liquidity and cash manipulate.

Accounts Receivable and Accounts Payable Aging: Keeps music of unpaid provider and customer invoices to help you in effectively dealing with receivables and payables.

Sales Reports: Examine your sales achievement thru way of purchaser, product, or issuer to have a examine greater about your top notch customers or satisfactory-promoting products.

Expense Reports: Classify and have a examine your industrial agency spending to help you find opportunities for charge-reducing or typical overall performance enhancements.

9.2 ADAPTING AND MEMORIZING REPORTS

QuickBooks permits you to comply reviews on your unique necessities and picks. The following is a way to customise and do not forget critiques in QuickBooks:

Open QuickBooks and select out the popular document.

Tailor the record on your wishes via converting the filters, date tiers, columns, and other settings.

The custom designed file may be stored with the aid of manner of choosing "Memorize" or "Save Customizations." By doing this, you could view the file within the future the use of the same settings.

Give the file a descriptive name and mean wherein you will want to maintain it for short get right of entry to.

You also can furthermore construct reviews in QuickBooks that deliver the right data you need, saving you time and effort, thru enhancing and remembering opinions.

9.Three EXAMINING KEY PERFORMANCE INDICATORS AND FINANCIAL STATEMENTS

It's critical to observe your QuickBooks evaluations as fast as you have got got created them to build up beneficial insights into the financial achievement of your corporation agency. Key average usual performance signs (KPIs) and economic statements evaluation examples are as follows:

Examine the steadiness sheet and profits and loss declaration to determine the profitability and liquidity of your agency.

To find out regions for development or trouble, check your financial statements to business agency benchmarks or historic statistics.

To observe the performance and economic viability of your company, compute and test important financial ratios along with the gross earnings margin, ROI, and modern ratio.

Track and compare KPIs relevant for your place or corporation targets, together with average order size, client acquisition fee, and employee overall performance.

You may additionally furthermore see styles, discover areas that need interest or development, and make nicely-knowledgeable choices to propel the boom of your organization via examining your economic money owed and key standard standard overall performance symptoms.

Making knowledgeable judgments approximately your agency's financial reputation is viable with the assist of QuickBooks' document generation and assessment features. You can also moreover efficiently look at the financial health of your employer and sell its growth and profitability thru the usage of the large style of QuickBooks opinions, personalizing and remembering them to fulfill your goals, and reviewing monetary statements and key common overall performance symptoms

Chapter 12: Advanced Features and Integrations

Advanced skills and integration options furnished with the resource of QuickBooks can similarly enhance your user experience and simplify your enterprise operations. Let's take a look at a few crucial factors of QuickBooks' superior abilties and integration:

10.1 WORKING WITH MULTIPLE USERS AND USER PERMISSIONS:

QuickBooks permits you to coordinate with severa clients and set fine man or woman permissions to restriction get proper of get right of entry to to to private monetary records. In QuickBooks, study the ones steps to have interaction with multiple customers and configure person permissions:

Create particular character payments for truly everyone who desires get right of access to to QuickBooks. Define their responsibilities and functions within the software program software software.

Customize person rights to allow or restrict access to unique QuickBooks areas and competencies. As a prevent end result, users will simplest have get entry to to responsibilities and information which might be pertinent to their employment.

Control Data Security: Implement the right individual rights to guard sensitive economic information and make certain that nice people with the right authorizations also can get right of entry to it.

You can encourage collaboration, uphold facts safety, and beautify regular workflow effectiveness thru way of jogging with many clients and defining individual rights in QuickBooks.

10.2 INTEGRATING QUICKBOOKS WITH THIRD-PARTY APPS:

You might also enlarge the functionality of QuickBooks and expedite your company techniques through integrating it with lots of zero.33-celebration apps. Here are a few times of approaches integration may fit:

Integrate QuickBooks with well-known charge processors to allow clean on-line payments and automate transaction statistics.

Connect QuickBooks on your eCommerce platform to have sales facts, inventory ranges, and customer facts mechanically synced.

CRM Systems: To improve the efficiency of your client dating control (CRM) system, integrate QuickBooks into it.

Time Tracking and Payroll Software: To automate worker time inputs, payroll processing, and tax computations, synchronize QuickBooks with time monitoring and payroll software program software program.

You may also moreover decrease guide statistics enter, decrease errors, and decorate operational overall performance in some unspecified time in the future of your corporation thru connecting QuickBooks with zero.33-birthday celebration applications.

10.Three USING QUICKBOOKS ONLINE APPS TO AUTOMATE TASKS:

A market of applications to be had through QuickBooks Online may additionally additionally automate and streamline plenty of operations, developing your productiveness. Here are a few suggestions for using QuickBooks Online apps:

Visit the QuickBooks App Marketplace to find quite some apps made to paintings flawlessly with QuickBooks Online. Explore the App Marketplace.

Choose Useful Apps: Decide which programs wonderful in shape your specific employer requirements, including time tracking, assignment manipulate, expenditure monitoring, or stock manipulate.

Install and Configure programs: After putting in the chosen programs, configure them thru your desires with the resource of following the setup instructions.

Take Advantage of Automation: Once the applications are related with QuickBooks Online, they may automate techniques, sync records, and provide more competencies to enhance workflow.

You can also automate monotonous operations, growth information accuracy, and get more functionality to streamline your industrial employer approaches via the use of QuickBooks Online programs.

You can beautify your QuickBooks experience and streamline your business enterprise business enterprise operations with the useful resource of making use of the advanced abilties and integration capabilities of QuickBooks, collectively with on foot with multiple customers and consumer permissions, integrating with 1/three-party programs, and the usage of QuickBooks Online apps. You may additionally moreover streamline your workflow, keep time, and enhance the effectiveness of monetary manipulate and industrial business enterprise operations by using tailoring this machine in your particular desires and connecting it with complementing solutions.

TROUBLESHOOTING AND ERROR-FIXING

Although QuickBooks is a dependable utility, occasionally errors and issues also can moreover rise up. You can greater successfully cope with any problems you run into in case you apprehend the way to troubleshoot common mistakes, repair data report troubles, and get help and manual. Let's have a observe some vital factors of QuickBooks mistake detection and restore:

11.1 TYPICAL QUICKBOOKS MISTAKES AND FIXES:

There are tremendous problems that you can run into even as using QuickBooks. Here are a few traditional QuickBooks errors and capability fixes:

Error 3371: When QuickBooks isn't capable of initialize the licensing houses, this error seems. This problem is usually steady with the aid of reinstalling and activating QuickBooks.

Error 6000 series: These errors, together with 6000 eighty three and 6000 seventy seven, regularly thing to problems with the business corporation report. These issues may additionally moreover often be ordinary thru the usage of the QuickBooks File Doctor device or through restoring a backup replica of the commercial enterprise record.

Error 12007: During QuickBooks updates, this mistake is established to issues with internet get admission to. To ensure that they'll be not restricting QuickBooks' capacity to connect with the internet, check your net connection, firewall configurations, and antivirus software software application.

Error 6123: This errors seems whilst restoring a backup or having access to a enterprise organisation document through a network. This errors may be consistent with the resource of the usage of the QuickBooks File Doctor software or thru manually repairing the community connection troubles.

It is usually endorsed to go to the reliable QuickBooks help internet web site or community boards for specific problem codes or messages for step-by using manner of-step troubleshooting instructions.

eleven.2 FIXING DATA FILE PROBLEMS:

Data document troubles may possibly compromise the reliability and accuracy of your QuickBooks statistics. Here are some strategies for troubleshooting information document troubles:

Verify and Rebuild Data: To check for and deal with information integrity issues, use the included Verify and Rebuild Data features in QuickBooks. These tools may additionally help in locating and solving data problems to your corporation record.

Condense Data: If the dimensions of your industrial organization corporation record has grown too large or it's far affecting performance, condense your facts. Condensing information in QuickBooks preserves the integrity of your economic facts on the same time as doing away with old transactions and shrinking the file length.

Restore from Backup: Restoring a present day backup replica of your employer report will help in statistics healing in case your document is corrupted or destroyed. To shield your records and permit healing in case of a disaster, you need to often another time up your company enterprise agency record.

Before starting any troubleshooting or information document-related duties, continuously ensure you have were given a latest backup of your company file.

11.Three RESOURCES FOR HELP AND SUPPORT SEEKING:

There are numerous web sites reachable for steerage and assist at the same time as the use of QuickBooks whilst encountering problems or wanting assistance:

Official QuickBooks Support: Go to the respectable QuickBooks useful resource net web site to accumulate FAQs, expertise base articles, and troubleshooting manuals. Depending for your QuickBooks subscription, the help internet website online furthermore offers cellular phone or live chat carrier.

QuickBooks Community: Sign up for the forums to community with specific QuickBooks customers and professionals. The network is a beneficial device for problem-fixing, enjoy-sharing, and finding answers to commonplace troubles.

Certified ProAdvisors: Think about getting into touch with QuickBooks-savvy Certified ProAdvisors. They also can offer individualized advice, practise, and assistance catered to the perfect requirements of your commercial enterprise business enterprise.

QuickBooks Help Menu: The QuickBooks utility has a Help menu that you could employ to find out context-touchy help, do trouble searches, and get admission to the QuickBooks Learning Center.

When requesting help, hold in thoughts to be as particular as possible about the error or problem you're experiencing because of the fact this could help with a extra precise evaluation and solution.

You can also moreover efficiently deal with problems and hold the steadiness and integrity of your QuickBooks records with the resource of way of being acquainted with traditional QuickBooks errors and their fixes, troubleshooting statistics report issues, and using the to be had assist and assist system. You can overcome stressful conditions and keep the use of QuickBooks for effective monetary manage because of its strong help gadget, which guarantees that assistance is continually reachable at the equal time as needed.

Chapter 13: Best Practices and Efficiency Optimization

Workflows ought to be streamlined, information backup and protection need to take delivery of priority, and high-quality practices need to be adhered to to get the maximum out of QuickBooks and make certain effective economic control. Let's have a observe a few vital elements of QuickBooks performance optimization and satisfactory practices:

12.1 SIMPLIFYING KEYBOARD SHORTCUTS AND WORKFLOWS:

When using QuickBooks, streamlining your techniques and using keyboard shortcuts can also greatly growth your productivity. Think approximately the subsequent advice:

Customize QuickBooks: By personalizing paperwork, templates, and evaluations, you can adapt QuickBooks to the proper requirements of your organization. You could be able to use the functions which may be maximum important on your operations quite absolutely way to this.

Automate repeated chores: Use QuickBooks' ordinary transactions, economic group feeds, and guidelines gadget to automate repeated chores. You'll shop time and do an lousy lot a good deal less guide statistics get entry to as a give up stop result.

Use Keyboard Shortcuts: To browse fast and complete not unusual sports extra effectively in QuickBooks, discover ways to use keyboard shortcuts. Ctrl + I, Ctrl + J, and Ctrl + W, as an instance, open the Create Invoice window, the Customer Center, and the present day window, respectively.

You might also additionally increase productivity and end sports in QuickBooks more rapid via optimizing your strategies and using keyboard shortcuts.

12.2 DATA BACKUP AND SECURITY PRECAUTIONS

It's vital to defend your QuickBooks data by way of using manner of doing not unusual backups and setting safety competencies in area. Consider the pinnacle recommendations underneath:

Regularly Back Up Your Data: Create automated backups of your QuickBooks corporation document to make sure that your statistics is safeguarded inside the case of a hardware malfunction, information corruption, or different unanticipated activities.

Store Backups Off-Site: Use cloud-based totally storage services or preserve backup copies of your organisation files in a safe off-website on-line area. This adds some other diploma of safety in opposition to bodily damage or theft.

Put User Access Controls in Place: In QuickBooks, you can assign patron rights to limit get right of entry to to personal monetary information. Review and update consumer permissions frequently to make sure that only people with the right get proper of get entry to to also can use a sure area or feature.

Use reliable anti-virus and anti-malware software at the laptop(s) walking QuickBooks: Install and keep this software software updated often. By doing this, you could protect your facts toward protection risks.

You can shield your QuickBooks information and reduce the opportunity of facts loss or illegal get proper of access to with the aid of giving records backup a excessive precedence and putting protection features in place.

12.Three ADVICE FOR MANAGING QUICKBOOKS ONLINE SUCCESSFULLY:

If you operate QuickBooks Online, endure in mind this management recommendation:

Use economic business enterprise feeds on your benefit via linking your financial business enterprise money owed to QuickBooks Online and the usage of them to import and classify transactions mechanically. To preserve accuracy, reconcile your bank debts frequently

Use Mobile applications: Download the QuickBooks Online cell packages for your tablet or cellular cellphone to send invoices, hold music of spending, and manage clients and vendors from everywhere.

Using Reports to Gain Insights Use QuickBooks Online to create and take a look at vital evaluations like Profit and Loss, Balance Sheet, and Cash Flow to collect insightful information about the financial health of your agency.

Work collectively together with your accountant to streamline monetary manipulate, benefit expert steering, and guarantee right tax submitting with the resource of sharing your QuickBooks Online statistics with them.

You can efficaciously manage your monetary data and get preserve of insightful information approximately the success of your employer through putting the ones suggestions into exercise and using the abilties provided with the resource of QuickBooks Online.

You can growth productivity, defend your records, and get the most out of QuickBooks through way of optimizing workflows, using keyboard shortcuts, prioritizing records backup and safety features, and adhering to brilliant practices for the control of QuickBooks Online. These techniques will will will let you control your charge variety efficaciously and give you the capacity to determine the way to make bigger and achieve your organization.

BEYOND THE FUNDAMENTALS

Once you are familiar with the fundamentals of QuickBooks, you may further enhance your revel in and get deeper insights into your commercial enterprise corporation's operations thru the use of the use of superior abilities and techniques. Let's take a look at a few contemporary QuickBooks recommendations and tips:

thirteen.1 ADVANCED CUSTOMIZATION OPTIONS:

To wholesome this system to your unique organisation necessities, QuickBooks offers superior customization alternatives. Think approximately the subsequent personalization alternatives:

Custom Fields: Use custom fields to accumulate extra information this is great for your enterprise. Custom fields can be made for customers, providers, merchandise, and more.

Advanced Reports Customization: Use the Advanced Customization alternatives to generate new reviews or alter contemporary ones. To deal with an appropriate records you want, trade the columns, filters, headers, and footers.

Importing specific templates: Use unique templates, which includes invoices or buy orders, to fit your commercial company's brand and deliver all of your files a unified look.

You may additionally tailor QuickBooks to meet your unique employer desires and decorate the person experience with the aid of using top notch customization capabilities.

thirteen.2 MEMORIZING TRANSACTIONS AND RECURRING TRANSACTIONS ARE COVERED:

You might also additionally store time and optimize your manner in QuickBooks with the aid of using memorizing and enforcing routine transactions. Think approximately the subsequent techniques:

Memorizing Transactions: For regularly occurring transactions, which consist of month-to-month lease or software program payments, memorize the transaction to have the data filled in robotically. By doing this, you could not ought to manually input the equal transaction extra than as soon as.

Create recurrent transactions to automate routine payments, invoices, and mag entries: You may additionally set the frequency, starting date, and ending date for the ones transactions, and QuickBooks will create them automatically primarily based in your particular time desk.

You may additionally additionally restrict guide statistics get right of access to and assure reliable and speedy execution of habitual transactions by means of the use of the reminiscence and repeating transaction competencies.

thirteen.Three MAKING USE OF CLASSES, LOCATIONS, AND JOB TRACKING:

In QuickBooks, training, locations, and machine tracking may additionally furthermore give you more in-depth facts at the performance and profitability of numerous components of your commercial enterprise. Think approximately the following techniques:

Classes: Classify transactions by using departments, product lines, or a few other pertinent standards via assigning schooling to them. This permits you to show overall performance through elegance, report on it, and get understanding about the profitability of numerous employer divisions.

Locations: Use the locations tool to song and take a look at general performance and costs for every internet web page independently in case your corporation has many places or branches.

Job Tracking: Use the interest tracking characteristic to assign cash, costs, and time to first-rate duties in case you paintings on duties or jobs. This makes it feasible if you want to hold song of the profitability of every challenge one after the other.

You may additionally additionally test the financial normal normal overall performance of numerous parts of your organization and make informed selections to increase profitability and performance via the use of utilizing instructions, places, and undertaking tracking in QuickBooks.

You may additionally moreover decorate your financial control with the resource of the usage of large customization alternatives, memorizing and repeating transactions, and the use of QuickBooks' lessons, locations, and project tracking capabilities. With the assist of those cutting-edge-day suggestions and techniques, you can customise QuickBooks to satisfy the specific wishes of your enterprise agency and make higher alternatives for enlargement and fulfillment. They also provide you with more insights and customization possibilities.

Chapter 14: Case Studies and Practical Examples

Case research and real-global examples display how a positive concept or solution abilties in sensible situations and provide insightful records. They entail searching at particular instances or businesses and demonstrating how requirements, strategies, or devices may be used to conquer obstacles or arrive at preferred consequences. Example research offer a thorough evaluation of a selected instance, consisting of the hassle, the answer, and the consequences, at the same time as actual-global examples deliver extra succinct motives of thoughts or strategies. Case studies and actual-worldwide examples are each superb analyzing equipment that show people how theories and practices may be located into exercise even as additionally motivating them with instances of actual-lifestyles success.

14.1 SETTING UP A SMALL BUSINESS WITH QUICKBOOKS ONLINE:

Let's have a examine an instance of a small enterprise setup in QuickBooks Online:

Hypothetical scenario: Sarah is setting up a modest on-line retail shop to provide handcrafted rings. Using QuickBooks Online, she desires to efficaciously manipulate her rate variety and keep track of her receipts and profits.

Solution: Sarah gadgets up her small commercial enterprise in QuickBooks Online by means of way of way of following those steps:

1. Create an Account and a Company: Sarah logs into QuickBooks Online and creates a modern day account. She offers the applicable statistics, together with her employer call, telephone amount, and region.

2. Adjust Company Settings: After setting up her agency, Sarah makes critical changes to the agency organization settings. She places up her tax settings, provides her logo, and aligns the chart of payments with the unique

income and charge streams for her organisation.

3. Connect Bank Accounts: Using the economic group feeds preference, Sarah links her commercial enterprise corporation's bank account to QuickBooks Online. As a result, she may moreover moreover combine her economic institution transactions into QuickBooks automatically and remove the want for human information access.

4. Create product and business enterprise devices in QuickBooks: Online to reflect your inventory of jewelry. Sarah does this. She inserts statistics which includes item names, descriptions, pricing, and stock levels.

five. Manage Customers and Sales: Sarah enters the names, touch records, and transport addresses of her customers into QuickBooks Online. After that, she generates and affords invoices to her customers for every transaction, keeping song of the gadgets bought and the sums owed.

6. Keep song of expenses: Sarah logs all of her out-of-pocket charges in QuickBooks Online. She divides expenses into pertinent money owed, along with those for assets, packaging, and advertising and marketing and marketing and advertising and marketing. For future reference, she also can be part of receipts or incredible workplace work.

7. Reconcile Bank Accounts: To make sure that the information in QuickBooks Online corresponds to her actual economic institution statements, Sarah reconciles her economic institution bills often. This allows her to keep precise monetary records and notice any anomalies or mistakes.

eight. Create Reports: Sarah creates evaluations like Profit and Loss, Sales thru Product/Service, and Accounts Receivable Aging using the reporting equipment in QuickBooks Online. These reviews supply her records at the financial success of her agency and beneficial useful aid in her choice-making.

Sarah might also additionally with out trouble manage her finances, have a look at her income and fees, and benefit beneficial insights into the operation of her small enterprise employer with the resource of putting in location her small business in QuickBooks Online and the use of its talents.

14.2 ADVANCED REPORTING FOR A SERVICE-BASED BUSINESS:

Let's check a actual-international example of advanced reporting in QuickBooks for a company-based business agency:

John, who owns a consulting commercial enterprise agency, wants to song key ordinary performance symptoms (KPIs), observe his company's financial facts, and make facts-pushed options to increase profitability.

Solution: John makes use of QuickBooks' large reporting capabilities to track his enterprise's monetary overall performance and accumulate insights:

1. Customizing Reports: John makes use of QuickBooks to customise reports so that they deliver attention to the precise statistics he desires to have a take a look at. To create reviews particularly for his corporation, he alters columns, gives filters, and chooses pertinent date intervals. He alters the Profit and Loss record, as an instance, to expose income and costs broken down through service kind.

2. Producing KPI Reports: John produces reviews that music KPIs unique to his consultancy business enterprise. He mentions stats much like the average earnings in line with customer, the charge of obtaining a patron, and the sort of billable hours normal with worker. John might also additionally music the general performance of his company and pinpoint opportunities for development via robotically reading the ones KPI evaluations.

3. Cash Flow Analysis: John analyzes his enterprise corporation's coins inflows and

outflows over a certain duration the usage of the Cash Flow Statement document in QuickBooks. He can control spending, and time with purchaser invoicing, and make sure there may be enough cash available via reading his cash go together with the flow styles.

four. Budgeting and Variance Analysis: To look at his actual monetary normal overall performance to the amounts expected, John creates budgets in QuickBooks. To study deviations and pinpoint areas in which he wants to adjust his spending or income-producing techniques, he creates charge range vs. Actual opinions.

five. Job Costing: John video display devices the monetary fulfillment of specific consulting obligations for the cause that his business enterprise is service-primarily based definitely absolutely. He analyzes work costing data from QuickBooks to decide the profitability of tasks, preserve song of task-related costs, and examine the general monetary achievement of every patron engagement.

6. Exporting and Sharing Reports: To percentage reviews along with his organisation, companions, or consumers, John exports critiques from QuickBooks. He can also edit the file headers and footers to embody his agency's brand and further records, and he can save opinions in a whole lot of formats which embody PDF or Excel.

John can also moreover moreover better apprehend the financial general overall performance of his consulting organization with the usage of QuickBooks' entire reporting equipment, song key universal normal overall performance symptoms, and make facts-driven selections an incredible manner to growth profitability and simple success.

Chapter 15: Future Trends and QuickBooks Online Updates

QuickBooks' internet platform and technology both hold to boom. Updates and upgrades to QuickBooks Online are regularly made to growth user revel in, provide new capabilities, and stay present day with fashion traits. Future dispositions and QuickBooks Online upgrades will consciousness on enhancing customer enjoy, boosting productivity, providing greater latest economic insights, and staying abreast of converting company requirements and organisation norms. Businesses can get the most out of QuickBooks Online for their economic control thru the use of adopting those modifications and remaining up to date with the newest talents.

15.1 EXAMINING THE MOST RECENT FEATURES OF QUICKBOOKS ONLINE

To enhance man or woman experience and supply businesses current financial manipulate tools, QuickBooks Online is normally evolving and which includes new capabilities. Here are some of QuickBooks Online's ultra-modern features:

1. Automated Sales Tax: QuickBooks Online now affords computerized earnings tax calculations, simplifying the computation and monitoring of profits tax for agencies. Based on the patron's area, it routinely calculates the ideal tax expenses and keeps song of any tremendous income tax.

2. Receipt Capture and Expense Tracking: Users of the QuickBooks Online cell app can also make use of the camera on their phone to take receipts whilst they're on the road. To make price monitoring easy, this machine robotically collects pertinent information, which incorporates provider call, date, and quantity.

3. Cash Flow Planner: By reading profits, spending, and previous banking transactions, QuickBooks Online's Cash Flow Planner gives an intensive attitude of a corporation's coins glide. It assists agencies in properly

forecasting and handling their coins go with the glide.

4. Project Profitability Tracking: QuickBooks Online now has superior alternatives for tracking project profitability. Users can successfully manipulate venture charges and profitability via allocating profits and spending to unique obligations.

five. Streamlined and additional effective economic institution feeds: had been added to QuickBooks Online, making them extra consumer-pleasant. Users can also classify transactions, hyperlink them with preexisting facts, and automate magnificence by way of way of way of putting in economic organization suggestions.

These are just a few instances of the maximum up to date QuickBooks Online abilties. New capabilities are regularly added because of the fact this gadget develops to satisfy the transferring desires of institutions.

15.2 ADJUSTING FOR CHANGES AND FUTURE IMPROVEMENTS

To increase capability, protection, and patron enjoy, QuickBooks Online mechanically offers updates and additions. Here are a few recommendations for adjusting to changes and getting ready for drawing near enhancements:

1. Stay Informed: Stay knowledgeable about adjustments to QuickBooks Online by using checking the professional QuickBooks internet internet site, signing up for product updates or newsletters, and using legit QuickBooks social media systems. By doing this, you may be knowledgeable as quick as new abilties and enhancements are available.

2. Investigate Training and Resources: Take use of the webinars, tutorials, and on-line guides that QuickBooks gives as education assets. By the usage of those device, you could ensure you're getting the most out of QuickBooks Online and find out about new competencies

3. Test New Features: Before introducing new functions in your stay organization record, keep in mind attempting out them in a controlled placing or the usage of a pattern commercial enterprise company file. This lets in you to turn out to be acquainted with the modifications and make certain they're well best alongside side your current strategies.

4. Offer Feedback: Don't be afraid to provide QuickBooks feedback if you run across any problems or have mind for enhancements. They recognize customer input and use it in their software application improvements to higher serve customers.

5. Get Involved within the Community: Join the QuickBooks man or woman boards or network to meet awesome clients, switch stories, and advantage records from each other. To test more about first-rate practices, insights, and advice from distinct QuickBooks Online customers, check out this useful aid.

You can also with out troubles modify to modifications and planned developments and maximize the advantages of QuickBooks Online through last informed approximately updates to QuickBooks Online, investigating training options, trying new functions, presenting comments, and connecting with the QuickBooks community.

It's vital to do not forget that the correct capabilities and improvements described here are based totally totally on the information I definitely have as of the facts cutoff date of September 2021. Beyond this period, QuickBooks Online must have introduced new functions and enhancements. Please seek advice from the reputable QuickBooks net website or get in touch with QuickBooks purchaser care for the most modern and correct statistics.

Chapter 16: Setting Up Your Chart of Accounts

You can installation and categorize the economic transactions of your enterprise in QuickBooks Online in your precise wishes by means of developing and enhancing your chart of debts.

Creating and customizing your chart of money owed

Here's the way to make your chart of money owed precise and layout it:

1). Log into QuickBooks Online and pick out the Gear icon in the pinnacle-proper corner of the UI to get right of access to the Chart of Accounts. Choose "Chart of Accounts" from the drop-down menu in the "Your Company" segment.

2). Add an Account: To upload a modern day account in your chart, click on the "New" button inside the pinnacle-proper nook of the Chart of Accounts page.

3). Choose the proper Account Type and Detail Type for the account you need to set up. The Detail Type offers more special classes internal each Account Type (e.G., Checking, Advertising Expense, Sales Income), at the same time as the Account Type suggests the general class of the account (e.G., Bank, Expense, Income).

four). Account Name and Number: Fill out the "Account Name" shape with the account's name. This need to be a succinct name that makes it smooth that permits you to apprehend the account. An optionally to be had unique account huge variety may be given to facilitate business enterprise employer and sorting.

5). You can tie the account to a selected tax line item, if relevant. This simplifies the tax reporting way. From the dropdown menu, pick out the proper tax line object.

6). Save the Account: To add and shop a brand new account to your chart of bills, click on at the "Save and Close" opportunity.

7). Customize Account association: Click and drag an account to the popular vicinity to your chart to trade the affiliation of the bills. This aids in arranging your chart of bills in a way that is practical on your enterprise.

8). Edit or Delete Accounts: To make changes to an present account, find out it inside the chart and choose the dropdown arrow next to it. You have the selection of improving, deactivating, or deleting the account from the alternatives provided.

9). Subaccounts: To further categorize and put together your financial records, QuickBooks Online also permits you to feature sub debts to your chart of bills. To create a subaccount, click the dropdown arrow next to an gift account and choose out out "New subaccount." Set up the subaccount the usage of the same strategies as above.

10). Account Hierarchy: By growing decide money owed and connecting sub payments to them, you could create a hierarchical form internal your chart of debts. This might also help in giving a clearer view of the economic instructions and connections for your enterprise.

eleven). You can also adapt the accounting framework to your organisation's wishes via constructing and customizing your chart of money owed in QuickBooks Online. This will make it much less complicated to because it must be manipulate and observe your economic sports activities activities. As your organisation grows, make sure your chart of payments is continuously reviewed and up to date to be consistent along with your goals for monetary reporting.

12). Your chart of bills in QuickBooks Online may be organized into training and subcategories to help you construct a logical form that fits your enterprise's economic reporting requirements. You can categorize your bills into one-of-a-type corporations the use of the following approach:

thirteen). Determine Account Categories: To begin, determine on the primary groups in order to function your bills' current classifications. Assets, Liabilities, Equity, Income, and Expenses are ordinary lessons. Consider the crucial economic additives, then classify the payments well.

14). Create decide debts to represent each magnificence for your chart of money owed. Follow the commands in the "Creating and Customizing Your Chart of Accounts" segment above to characteristic a determine account.

15). Account types and element sorts want to be because it ought to be assigned to every parent account. This ensures that the decide account is given the right type. For example, an Equity determine account will include Owner's Equity or Retained Earnings as a appropriate Detail Type similarly to Equity due to the fact the Account Type.

16). You can create sub bills interior every decide account to further categorize and installation your debts. Subaccounts provide more detail and precision. You will have sub money owed like Advertising Expense, Rent

Expense, or Office Supplies Expense within the Expense determine account, for instance.

17). Link Sub Accounts to Parent Accounts: When installing a sub account, make certain to connect it to the proper determine account. This ensures that the subaccount is nested below the proper class and permits construct the hierarchical hyperlink.

18). Set Account Numbers: Giving your debts account numbers permit you to arrange and classify them better. Account numbers may be added while growing new bills or thru enhancing ones that exist already. It may be much less hard to find out and recognize bills inside every elegance in case you use a logical numbering scheme (as an instance, a thousand for property and 2000 for liabilities).

19). Regularly have a observe your chart of money owed and make any critical changes. You may additionally want to feature new debts, alter modern-day ones, or make new instructions and subcategories as your business enterprise develops. Make fantastic the shape meets your desires for financial reporting and offers the quantity of element required for specific assessment.

A logical and obvious shape for monitoring and evaluating your monetary statistics is furnished thru categorizing and subcategorizing your debts. It makes accurate reporting less complex, makes statistics get entry to a lot much less difficult, and makes it much less complicated to understand precise account kinds. You'll have better visibility into your enterprise organization's financial basic overall performance and be capable of make greater knowledgeable selections in case you hold your chart of debts organized.

Understanding the impact of chart of money owed on financial reporting

The basis for arranging and classifying monetary transactions internal an accounting device like QuickBooks Online, the chart of payments performs a important position in financial reporting.

The chart of debts has the following essential results on economic reporting:

1). The chart of money owed makes tremendous that financial transactions are efficiently documented and classified in the proper debts. A tremendous magnificence, along side property, liabilities, fairness, sales, or charges is represented through every account in the diagram. The chart of money owed serves as the muse for growing accurate monetary statements and critiques thru because it want to be classifying transactions.

2). Financial Statement Preparation: The layout and records contained in monetary statements are strongly stimulated by way of way of the chart of money owed. Based at the information within the chart of money owed, the earnings statement, balance sheet, and assertion of cash flows are produced. The tool can aggregate and summarize sports activities activities into these economic statements manner to properly categorizing and organizing the money owed. This gives users a thorough understanding of the organization's economic performance, role, and coins flows.

3). Consistency and Comparability: A well-designed and meticulously saved chart of payments permits accurate comparisons among severa intervals and financial reporting periods. You might also take a look at dispositions, spot patterns, and maintain tabs on adjustments in economic information via routinely the usage of the equal instructions and payments over the years. It ensures consistency in reporting requirements and makes benchmarking closer to company norms or business desires an awful lot less hard.

four). Management Reporting and Analysis: A framework for generating first rate control reports and analyses is supplied thru the chart of money owed. You can also show and analyze financial universal overall performance through department, project, or product line by categorizing payments into full-size classes and extra specific subcategories that correspond to particular commercial enterprise business enterprise operations or fee facilities. This aids manipulate in choice-making, green beneficial resource allocation, and analysis of the profitability of severa business agency segments.

5). Compliance and Regulatory Reporting: Numerous regulatory groups and taxing government name for that organizations offer specific financial evaluations within the proper formats. The chart of debts affords the appropriate classifications and classes desired for these evaluations, ensuring compliance. Businesses can rapidly and effectively whole their reporting dreams via matching the chart of money owed with regulatory necessities.

Chapter 17: Transaction Recording

For accurate financial tracking and reporting, income and spending need to be entered and labeled in QuickBooks Online.

Entering and categorizing profits and fees

In QuickBooks Online, you may input and categorize earnings and fees as follows:

1). Income Generating Categories

Choose "Chart of Accounts" from "Your Company" through using the usage of selecting the Gear picture in the pinnacle-right nook.

To upload a logo-new account, click on the "New" button.

Select "Income" as the Account Type, then select a Detail Type this is suitable for the shape of earnings (collectively with Sales of Product Income or Service Fee Income).

Give the account a unique name and quantity, then store the account.

2). Data Entry for Income Transactions

Select "Sales" from the menu on the left.

You can input a positive form of earnings transaction thru choosing it, which include "Invoice" or "Sales Receipt".

Include all pertinent facts, which consist of purchaser information, the date, the gadgets or services sold, and the sums.

Select the right earnings category which you described in Step 1 under the "Account" column.

Examine the transactional statistics, then preserve it.

three). Making Expense Category Definitions

To get right of access to the Chart of Accounts, repeat step 1 commands.

To add a brand-new account, click on the "New" button.

Select "Expense" because the Account Type, and then choose a Detail Type that is appropriate for the sort of spending (e.G., lease rate, advertising and marketing and advertising and marketing and marketing price).

Give the account a completely unique call and big range, then hold the account.

4). Entering Transactions for Expenses

The "Expenses" link may be located on the left menu.

Choose "Expense" or "Check" relying at the sort of fee transaction you need to go into.

Include all applicable information, which include dealer statistics, the date, the outline, and the quantity.

Choose the best spending magnificence you described in Step 3 in the "Account" column.

Examine the transactional information, then store it.

5). Transaction Categorization: To guarantee right reporting, you could categorize gift transactions in addition to choosing the correct income or fee class whilst inputting transactions:

Select "Chart of Accounts" beneath the "Accounting" desire in the left menu.

Find the transaction inside the account join up which you need to categorize.

To view the transaction's information, click on on on it, then select out "Edit."

Select the right elegance for charges or profits within the "Category" segment.

To nicely classify the transaction, store the changes.

By often classifying earnings and charges in QuickBooks Online, you could make sure that your monetary information are correct, as a way to will let you produce precise opinions and get insightful expertise about the monetary health of your employer.

Utilizing monetary group feeds to reconcile and song your commercial enterprise agency transactions

Tracking and reconciling your industrial enterprise transactions is brief and clean with QuickBooks Online's bank feed characteristic. Through financial institution feeds, you could link your financial institution and credit score card money owed with QuickBooks Online to allow transaction import that takes place automatically.

Here are some tips for maximizing bank feeds:

1). Associated Bank Accounts

Click "Banking" inside the QuickBooks Online left navigation menu.

To begin connecting your bank account, click the "Connect Account" or "Add Account" desire.

To establish a robust connection, look for your monetary group or one-of-a-kind financial organization and enter your login records.

To authorize the connection and offer QuickBooks Online get right of entry to to your transaction statistics, adhere to the on-show commands.

2). Bank Transaction Import

Your financial group transactions might be right away imported into the "Banking" tab of QuickBooks Online as speedy as your economic group account is connected.

Examine the importation of transactions out of your monetary group account. To speed up the reconciliation machine, QuickBooks Online will take the time to healthful gift transactions, in conjunction with invoices or expenses.

3). Banking Transaction Reconciliation

Go to the "Banking" page and choose out the account you need to reconcile to reconcile your bank transactions.

Each transaction need to be tested and in evaluation to the matching get admission to in your financial group declaration.

To display that the transactions had been reconciled, mark them as "Reviewed" or "Matched". Any unrivaled transactions moreover can be manually reconciled via way of selecting them and taking the essential movement.

4). Matching and Categorizing Transactions

Choose the correct income or spending elegance to categorize transactions that aren't proper now matched to current facts.

Create recommendations in QuickBooks Online to routinely classify repeating transactions in line with predetermined necessities.

Use QuickBooks Online's "Find Match" device to search for viable fits among imported transactions and modern-day information.

five). New Transactions Adding

By deciding on the "Add" button under the "Banking" tab in QuickBooks Online, you can manually add any transactions that are not covered inside the financial group feed.

Assign the proper earnings or spending elegance after moving into the transaction's specifics, which ought to encompass the date, sum, and description.

6). Examining and Making Up Discrepancies

Review your financial group feeds frequently and reconcile transactions to spot any inconsistencies or errors.

If there are any variations amongst your economic group announcement and the transactions in QuickBooks Online, have a look at them and be part of them.

If there are any questions about a transaction, get in contact in conjunction with your monetary group or certainly one of a kind monetary business enterprise.

You may additionally boost up the reconciliation method, limit human facts access, and assure particular tracking of your business enterprise's transactions with the useful resource of the usage of financial institution feeds in QuickBooks Online. You may additionally moreover more effortlessly manipulate your employer enterprise's budget by manner of frequently inspecting and reconciling your financial institution feeds because of the fact you will have updated, correct financial facts at your disposal.

Creating and handling invoices, sales receipts, and buy orders

To track income, record customer bills, and manage purchases on your organisation, you need to create and control invoices, income receipts, and purchase orders in QuickBooks Online.

The following outlines the manner to make and address the ones documents:

1). Producing Bills

Click "Sales" and then "Invoices" on the left menu to get admission to the invoices segment.

To create a ultra-modern bill, click the "New Invoice" button.

Include any pertinent facts, which include the client's name, billing cope with, bill date, and due date.

Add the products or services given to the customer, collectively with their quantities and fees. The totals may be calculated automatically through using QuickBooks Online.

Add a logo, use a template, or add a few specific phrases or messages to customise the bill.

Click "Save and deliver" to post the invoice to the patron or "Save and near" to store it for later after reviewing it.

2). Invoice manipulate

Go to the "Sales" internet page and select "Invoices" to view and manipulate cutting-edge-day invoices.

You can use the search scenario to look for individual invoices or clear out the invoices primarily based mostly on their reputation (open, late, paid).

To check an bill's records, make adjustments, or resend it to the patron, click on on on the bill.

By choosing the "Receive Payment" preference, you can mark an invoice as paid as speedy as the patron can pay it.

3). Receipting Sales

Sales receipts are used to record any payments made right away by using using clients for devices or services.

Select "Sales Receipts" from the "Sales" alternative at the left of the display show display screen.

To create a new sales receipt, use the "New Sales Receipt" button.

Include the decision of the customer, the payment method, and some different facts.

The gadgets or services provided, at the component of the associated sums, are added.

Click "Save and deliver" to ship a replica of the income receipt to the customer after reviewing it, or "Save and close to" to shop a duplicate to your information.

four). Establishing Purchase Orders

Orders placed with agencies are requested through buy orders, which can be then tracked.

www.ingramcontent.com/pod-product-compliance
Lightning Source LLC
Chambersburg PA
CBHW071222210326
41597CB00016B/1905